COPING WITH

An Unplanned

Pregnancy

An Unplanned

Pregnancy

Carolyn Simpson

THE ROSEN PUBLISHING GROUP, INC./NEW YORK

Published in 1990, 1994 by The Rosen Publishing Group, Inc.
29 East 21st Street, New York, NY 10010

Copyright 1990, 1994 by Carolyn Simpson

Revised Edition 1994

Library of Congress Cataloging-In-Publication Data

Simpson, Carolyn.
    Coping with an unplanned pregnancy / Carolyn Simpson.
        p.   cm.
    Includes bibliographical references
    Summary: Discusses the emotions, stresses, and adjustments
connected with an unplanned teenage pregnancy.
    ISBN 0-8239-1815-7
        1. Teenage mothers—United States—Juvenile literature.
    2. Teenage pregnancy—United States—Juvenile literature.
    3. Birth control—United States—Juvenile literature.
    [1. Pregnancy. 2. Teenage parents.] I. Title.
HQ759.4.S57   1990
306.85′6—dc20
                                                            89-70165
                                                               CIP
                                                                AC

Manufactured in the United States of America

ABOUT THE AUTHOR ◇

Carolyn Simpson, a teacher and writer, has worked in the mental health field since 1973. She received a Bachelor's Degree in Sociology from Colby College, Waterville, Maine, and a Master's Degree in Human Relations from the University of Oklahoma, Norman, Oklahoma.

She worked as a clinical social worker for ten years, both in Maine and Oklahoma, and as a teacher and counselor in the Young Parent's Program (serving pregnant teens) in Bridgton, Maine. Currently, she teaches Psychology at Tulsa Junior College in Tulsa, Oklahoma.

She has written several other books in this series, including *Coping with Teenage Motherhood* and *Coping with Emotional Disorders*. She lives with her husband and their three children on the outskirts of Tulsa.

For
Diane Hardersen and Nicholas,
who showed me that not
all unplanned pregnancies
are unwelcome!

Acknowledgments

Without the help of many people in the community, this book would not have been possible. I am deeply indebted to Olivia Casey-Jewett and Barbara Cohen, who head the Young Parents' Group in Bridgton, Maine, for their support and frankness in discussing their "girls," and to the "girls" themselves: Tina, Theresa, Barb, and Elissia, who willingly shared some of their feelings with me.

I am also indebted to Laurene Bercume, director of the Parenting Center at Bonny Eagle High School in West Buxton, Maine, for her help and guidance. Thanks too to her "kids": Bruce, Gina, and Phyllis, for sharing their stories.

Many thanks to Mary Hubka for her advice and for leading me to so many other helpful people, among them: Sally Dunning, R.N., an O.B. nurse at Northern Cumberland Memorial Hospital; Nancy Newsom Farmer, a guidance counselor at Lake Region High School in Naples, Maine; and Kathy Calder of the Family Planning Clinic in Augusta, Maine.

To my friends and colleagues—Sallie Clote, Director of Social Services at Norman Regional Hospital, Norman, Oklahoma; Georgia Ann Gibson, medical social worker at Hillcrest Medical Center, Tulsa; Helen Boyd, a psychologist in Oklahoma City; Deb Goepel, R.N., of Bridgton, Maine; Marcia Goodwin and her son, Chris, of Norman—I send special thanks and a hug.

Although I can never name you all (and for this book have disguised your situations and identities), I am thankful to all my past clients who have "educated" me along the way.

To the people behind the scenes: Sondra Shehab and Helen Boyd (for their long-distance words of encouragement), and to my children: Michal, Jaime, and Jarrett (who stopped fighting long enough for me to write and type this book), I am truly grateful.

But most of all, I want to thank my husband, Dwain, who supported, applauded, and encouraged me all along the way and on countless times took over my chores so I could finish this book on schedule. For you, Dwain, thanks and love . . .

Contents

Preface

It is estimated that in 1993 one million teenagers will become pregnant, resulting in 406,000 abortions, 134,000 miscarriages, and 490,000 births (over half to unwed mothers). These numbers seem less shocking today because they have held steady over the last few years. What *is* alarming is the number of girls fifteen and younger who are becoming pregnant. Teenage pregnancy is affecting a much younger crowd. Will this trend affect the options available?

THE IMPACT OF AN UNPLANNED PREGNANCY

Why do so many teenagers end up pregnant when schools are providing sex education and (in some cases) condoms? Researchers suspect that some teenagers *want* to get pregnant. School guidance counselors and psychologists have identified many "girls at risk" as being academic underachievers or as suffering from learning problems. Naturally, under those circumstances, school becomes an endless ordeal of failing to measure up and continually falling behind. Facing difficulties (whether in school or at home), teens sometimes look to motherhood to solve the stress in their lives. Motherhood is supposed to be something they can do well. Unfortunately, it is usually more than girls bargain for. One of my former students wrote me this letter when she learned she was pregnant again at barely seventeen.

"I have so many responsibilities now: changing diapers, making bottles, buying baby food, and buying baby clothes for the baby.

"A lot of times when my daughter is asleep, I think about things I used to do (and miss) before I had her. Things like staying out all night, cruising, having fun with my boyfriend, being able to come and go as I pleased, and not having to budget my money.

"I never had to worry about when the next feeding was due, or how I would con my Mom into baby-sitting because I needed a break.

"When I was little I used to think about growing up and having a baby of my own. It's a lot different in reality than it was as a thought. In my thoughts I was a wealthy woman, living in a mansion, with a baby and a gorgeous husband. In reality I live in a tiny two-bedroom apartment. I have to scrounge for money to buy diapers, and I love my boyfriend (her father) but he isn't a prince.

"Before I got pregnant, I was drinking a lot and into cocaine. When I found out I was pregnant, I realized it was time to grow up and face my responsibilities. I wasn't a little child anymore.

"I am happy with my daughter, and kind of happy with having another baby. I only wish I was older, and they could have waited a while longer."

Motherhood is difficult, and **teenage** motherhood even more so. Rarely is it as delightful as we dream it will be.

This book is intended, however, not to lecture those of you who are already pregnant, but rather to show you that:

1. you have many choices ahead, and . . .
2. if you choose to raise your baby, lots of help is available. You do not have to go through this alone! Motherhood may not be as "delightful" as you envisioned it, but it doesn't have to be the end of the world, either.

WHAT'S IN THIS BOOK

As you can see from the Contents, this book is in four parts. The first section discusses your options, of which you have only four: abortion, adoption (or temporary foster care), marriage, and single parenthood. There's something to be said for each of them, but remember that *you* are the one who has to make the decision. Doing nothing about your situation does not change the fact you're pregnant.

The second section looks at what can happen to your education, your friends, and your family when you're pregnant—not to mention how you might be feeling about such a momentous event.

Since approximately 406,000 teenagers choose to have abortions and another 134,000 lose their babies through miscarriage, the third section discusses losses: how it feels (I've suffered such a loss myself) and what you can do to survive it. Motherhood itself involves losses, and even when you're happy with your baby, you can still feel twinges of jealousy that your own childhood is over.

Last is a section describing the most important part: giving birth and taking the baby home. When you have some idea what to expect (during labor and later on at home), your're in better control. There's nothing worse than feeling "out of control." After all, you can't call the show off when you're in the middle of labor.

If you're reading this book as part of a sex education class, be sure to read the questions in the Appendix. If you're going to be sexually active, you need to be responsible. Better to consider your behavior before it puts you into an unplanned situation.

P A R T   ◇   I

A LOOK AT THE OPTIONS

CHAPTER 1

Marriage

Days have gone by. Too many days, in fact. Your period is a week late. Two weeks. You think back on those times your boyfriend told you it was safe, that you didn't need to use anything because he had never made anyone pregnant before and was probably sterile. You remember that time you thought it was okay not to bother with birth control. After all, you were *never ever* going to "do it" again, and surely this one time wouldn't make you pregnant. Or you remember thinking that time that douching afterward would wash away all the sperm.

Well, whatever the scenario, here you are. Your period is late, your breasts are aching, you can't stand the smell of bacon cooking in the morning, and you want this whole mess to just go away.

Let me tell you, you can drive yourself crazy worrying about what's going to happen with your life now. The same is true if you try to ignore all the signs, because ostrich-like behavior only limits your choices as the pregnancy progresses.

What you have to do first is determine that you actually *are* pregnant. You can buy one of the home pregnancy tests (which are accurate and quick, though not especially cheap); you can have a test done (often free of charge) at a family planning clinic; or you can see your personal physician for a more expensive assessment.

A drawback to the home testing method is that you're alone. If the test is positive, you don't have an informed person sitting there ready to outline your options. Family planning clinics (as long as they consider all choices equally) are good places to begin. A good clinic will not only detect the pregnancy but also link you with resources (for financial assistance, shelter, and counseling), whether or not you continue the pregnancy.

I assume, though, that if you've picked up this book and are reading it you already know you're pregnant. Just bear with me one more time: If you only suspect you're pregnant, check it out *now*. It won't go away by itself, and putting off facing the fact will only limit your eventual choices.

In the "old days" (as my daughter refers to the days of *my* youth—twenty years ago), if a girl found herself pregnant she got married. Pure and simple. She kept the baby, she dropped out of school, she probably ended up divorced with three kids under five, but she did the "right thing" for appearance's sake. Several girls in my high school class mysteriously dropped out of school in their junior year. None of us discussed it out loud, but we all wondered in private if they had had any fun...

Bonnie's boyfriend in high school was having trouble with his own folks, so he moved in with Bonnie's family. He had his own room downstairs, but gradually Bonnie's parents noticed less and less how much time the two were spending together. Bonnie liked being with Jerome...and not going to different houses after a date. Soon they became sexually active without considering the consequences. Bonnie later admitted that since they had always planned to marry, a pregnancy just didn't seem to be a significant issue.

Bonnie did become pregnant. She was stunned, not believing that it would actually happen after all. Sometimes she tried to "wish it away," but when she finally accepted the pregnancy she and her boyfriend chose to get married. "It was the right thing to do," she said later. Bonnie was most afraid to tell her father; she had always been "Daddy's girl," and she thought she was letting him down by dropping out of school and marrying the first man with whom she had been intimate. But despite the letdown of the unplanned pregnancy, Bonnie was certain marriage would make it more acceptable.

Some teenagers are angry or embarrassed when they "get caught." For one thing—and I was a teenager once, though a long time ago—it's hard to believe that anything bad will ever happen to you. You've heard all the lectures about birth control and sexually transmitted diseases, not to mention AIDS, but somehow those things don't touch you as they might other adults. Becoming pregnant, finding out that you're mortal or your parents are—these things are like slaps in the face. Unexpected. Naturally you get angry because after all, it just isn't fair...

Embarrassment isn't the issue it was back in my day. Back then, kids were alarmed at being pregnant because then everyone knew they'd been "doing it." All of us "good girls" were shocked to learn of so-and-so, who had obviously been putting out while we were keeping our sexual impulses under lock and key. Some of us may even have envied them experiencing something that we had yet to experience. But back then, embarrassment—and its cousin, guilt—were powerful deterrents to the rest of us.

For teenagers now, embarrassment probably comes

from feeling naive and irresponsible in not believing you can get pregnant.

So here you are: angry and embarrassed that you didn't beat the odds, and now you're going to be a mother at the age of fifteen, sixteen, or whatever. You love the guy; furthermore, you love babies, and you two had always planned to marry—just at a more opportune time. What you decide to do now is push up the wedding a little.

Some of you, despite all the anger, embarrassment, and misgivings, may also be feeling relieved that a wedding will take place. And perhaps excitement at having conceived.

A sixteen-year-old girl, Deborah, came in to see one of my friends for counseling. Originally it was because of family problems. Midway through the year, Deborah took up with another troubled teen, a boy a year or so older. One afternoon Deborah burst into the therapist's office. "I'm pregnant," she announced, the pride evident in her voice. When the therapist tried to probe beyond the initial enthusiasm, Deborah could only admit that this was an accomplishment of hers—a way for her to be like her older sisters, like the adult women in her family.

Another young woman said to me, "I wanted to be pregnant. I loved being pregnant. The sense of having something inside of me that belonged to no one else for nine months but me."

Weddings are supposed to be happy events, but sometimes marriages aren't "made in Heaven," as the saying goes. The odds are not in favor of your staying together, mostly because people do a lot of changing (growing up) in their early twenties. It takes a really committed, mature person to make the sacrifices needed to maintain a relationship and a family. Just look around you. The adults aren't doing such a great job in that department either.

When *anyone* marries today, he or she stands a fifty-fifty chance of getting divorced.

At some point during all the excitement of the wedding preparations, you might find yourself feeling "down" or sad or just plain scared. Those feelings don't necessarily mean that you don't want to be married. Sometimes an event as significant as this sobers you to the point of thinking about what you're getting into. While you may be perfectly thrilled to be marrying the guy you love, you realize too that you're giving up some things. No longer will society view you as a child. You will be a married woman, about to become a mother with all the attendant responsibilities. The focus is going to shift soon from *you* to the *infant* you're carrying. And even when the newness wears off, you're still going to have to live with this guy, be a wife, be a mother, pay bills.

All of which is simply to say that second thoughts aren't necessarily bad. Listen to them, because they're reminding you that life isn't going to be easy and what you are undertaking is important. But don't base a change of heart on feeling "blue" for a while. It's a normal feeling. The night before my own wedding—and I was a matronly twenty-eight at the time—I went to bed depressed. "Did I really think this through enough?" I kept asking myself.

After ten years of marital (dis)harmony, I know that if I had the opportunity I'd do it all over again in a second.

A former client had an unhappy experience with her own wedding. René had never aspired to a career. All she ever wanted out of life was the love of a good husband and several babies to raise. When she became pregnant at seventeen, it wasn't the end of the world. She had completed high school months before and knew she was involved with the man she wanted to marry. Unfortunately, as supportive as her parents were, they were ashamed of her pregnancy and just wanted the wedding to take place with as little fanfare as possible.

Fearing that others were probably shaking their heads in disapproval, they sacrificed René's early excitement for a rushed ceremony. René, whose dream had always included the big church wedding, the white dress, and the pile of presents, had to be content with a ceremony conducted in her home. Her father walked her across the living room instead of down the aisle at church. Only sisters and brothers and aunts and uncles witnessed the event. More distant family members were notified only afterward.

René, who is an unusally perceptive teenager, said to me later, "By treating the whole ceremony so casually, they gave me the impression that I was being punished. That if I'd done things right, they would have gone out of their way to give me a big wedding. As it turned out, I felt like a criminal. Doing something really dirty. So dirty that we couldn't invite the other relatives to watch it. Most of my family gave us wedding presents, but it wasn't the same as having a surprise shower. I felt the disapproval that came with every gift.

"For a long time afterward I was really mad at my parents. I mean, you'd have thought they'd be understanding. After all, they had to get married themselves. I guess they just expected better of me. There, see? I'm starting to believe it myself: that I did something wrong or could have done better. I love my husband, and I already love this baby. What's so awful about that?"

Then again, sometimes the fancy wedding does take place. You get tons of presents, you're the focus of activity for days leading up to the big event, and then of course the center of attention on the day itself. It's enough to make you lose sight of the fact that you're still pregnant and have all that to deal with. The honeymoon is a weekend in another town in the ritziest hotel your Dad can afford, and then on Monday reality hits when everyone starts planning for the baby. There's hardly any period of adjustment to married life. First there are the Lamaze classes so you both know what's what during childbirth, and then there's your mother telling you all the little things you need for a baby, including why drawstring-tied nightgowns are better than sleepers. Suddenly, there you are. Barely a couple and with plans for a baby. It's hard not to feel cheated or jealous. Cheated for missing out on other "couple" activities. And jealous of this new life growing inside you.

FROM THE MAN'S POINT OF VIEW

Not all guys faint or wither away when the topic of marriage comes up. While I've certainly seen many more guys who felt they were too young to get married, some have gone to extraordinary measures to fulfill responsibilities. Wayne was a young guy who worked with me at a hospital a few years ago. He had what I call the "rescuer mentality."

Wayne hadn't dated much in high school. The ward clerk at the hospital—a girl of eighteen—became pregnant, and her boyfriend evaporated into thin air. Wayne started dating Nancy, even when others warned him that she might accuse him of being the father. When Nancy was waddling around in the last stages of pregnancy, Wayne asked her to marry him. He had almost forgotten that the baby wasn't his in his determination to take responsibility for all of them. They married, Nancy quit work to stay home with the baby, and after delivery Wayne was so proud, you'd have thought he had done all the work himself.

Ed was another young man I knew. He was dating a girl a year older than himself, and when she went off to college one fall, he said, "If anything happens and you get pregnant or anything, you don't have to worry. I'll marry you in a second."

Very supportive words coming from a young guy who was still in high school and had his college years ahead of him. The ironic thing was that he wasn't necessarily referring to her getting pregnant by *him*. No matter how she wound up in that condition, Ed was willing to assume all responsibility. My own hunch is that Ed was caught up in the role of "knight in shining armor." He had no concept of how hard it is to finish high school, to work to pay bills, to love a woman (who might have been made pregnant by somebody else), and then to support her child.

Some guys actually want to settle down, but it's a safe bet that more do not want to burden themselves with a wife and child when they haven't finished high school.

For you guys, perhaps it isn't an issue of making your best girl pregnant. Perhaps it was a two-week affair with a girl you soon realized you did not care that much about. Unfortunately, the relationship progressed so quickly that intimacy developed before caring and love. In that case, the mere thought of marriage might turn your knees to jelly. There just is no single way a guy is bound to feel about a shotgun wedding.

Marriage is an option for the couple in which the girl finds herself unexpectedly pregnant. But it is not necessarily the *only* one, nor the *best*. It is viable only if both people really want to commit themselves to each other for the next fifty or so years. Think about it. People are living well into their seventies and eighties, which means that the guy you marry at sixteen will be facing you across the dinner table for another fifty-four years or more. If you're thinking of marriage as a temporary measure to remedy a night of irresponsible sexual activity, you're in for a rude awakening.

Divorce, even when the marriage is not worth staying in, feels *terrible*. It hurts. It hurts to give up on something, on someone you once cared about. It's scary to realize that you're going to be back playing dating games again, getting to know someone, hoping it will all work out. Not to mention worrying over whether or not your ex will come through with the support money this month.

But if your decision to marry is grounded in reality, by all means formalize your relationship. Later I'll share some extraordinary stories of teens who married and beat the odds.

But for now, what if there isn't the option to marry? What if you're involved with an older man or a married man, both of whom may be unavailable. What if you discovered you were pregnant after being raped? Or submitting to sex with a relative? (There's nothing that says incest won't result in pregnancy.) What if you're not even sure who the father is?

When marriage isn't the logical choice, you'll have to do some soul-searching and come up with an alternative. Read on for a discussion of the other choices: abortion, adoption or temporary foster care, and single parenthood.

Remember: Not making a choice is choosing to have the baby.

CHAPTER 2

Deciding on

Abortion

During the past couple of years, the courts have attempted to overturn the 1973 Supreme Court ruling legalizing abortion (known as *Roe* v. *Wade*) or to severely restrict its application, state by state. Until 1993, they had succeeded in making abortions more difficult to obtain. Despite the controversy, however, remember that *abortion is still legal.*

Because of the election of President Bill Clinton, who favors a woman's right to choose, we shall see significant changes regarding abortion. In recent years, the pro-life movement has gained considerable momentum, its goal being to get the Supreme Court to outlaw abortion. To that end, militants have marched on abortion clinics, harassing both the people seeking abortions and the doctors who perform the procedure. During the past twelve years, pro-life advocates succeeded in curtailing many of the rights *Roe* v. *Wade* originally insured. As recently as December 1992, a federally funded clinic would not have been able to give you abortion information or even referral to an agency that would offer the information. On January 22, 1993, President Clinton removed the gag order on providing abortion information and referral at clinics that received government funds. You now have more options than you did a year ago. Nevertheless, you need to remember two things. Controversy rages on both sides of the abortion issue; since Dr. David Gunn was shot and killed for performing abortions in March 1993, many people will be hesitant to take his place. For you, that means it may be harder to get the service you desire. Second, many states now restrict abortion. You may be required to tell your parents (or husband) before seeking an abortion; you may be required to wait twenty-four hours before the procedure can be done. DON'T LET THESE RESTRICTIONS DETER YOU IF THIS IS THE OPTION YOU CHOOSE. If you happen to live in such a state, you can drive to a state that does not have these restrictions. You can also seek the court's permission to have the abortion without informing your parents (usually only granted in cases of abusive relationships). Or, you can inform your parents. Stalling solves nothing; it merely removes your options.

Informing your parents need not mean the end of the world. Often, they do not react as badly as you fear. In the event, though, that you're seriously upset about their possible reactions, you can get workers at a family planning clinic to help you break the news. Most parents would rather know (and thus be of support to you) than to leave such an important decision in your hands alone.

A young woman came to see my colleague following rape by her stepfather and subsequent abortion. Philosophically Sara had been dead set against abortion, but then she wasn't expecting the father of her stepbrothers to become the father of her baby. One evening when she was home alone, her stepfather raped her. When Sara later discovered she was pregnant, she was so overwhelmed with disgust that she scheduled an immediate abortion. She never told her family.

Sara told her counselor, "I never thought I'd be one to have an abortion. I never meant to, and I don't feel so great about what I did. I try to think of it simply as my stepfather's kid. It wasn't right, what he did to me. That baby wasn't conceived in love or even in a moment of lust. It wasn't *my* mistake. Why should I have had to live with that the rest of my life?"

Another woman I met recently described why she had had an abortion. Mary was seventeen when her first child was born. A family crisis had been brewing for some time, and Mary had attempted to deal with it by risking a pregnancy with her boyfriend. Mary chose not to marry her boyfriend. She remained at home with her parents (who were supportive although embarrassed by the circumstances), and she ultimately delivered a lovely little girl she named Cindy. Her parents help with child care, and Mary returned to high school to get her diploma.

A year after Cindy was born, Mary became pregnant again. This time she couldn't bear to tell her parents or even her boyfriend. She went alone to a clinic and had the abortion. When I talked with Mary—several months after the abortion—I was struck by her unacknowledged guilt. She kept saying, "It was no big deal." In fact, she probably said that twelve times in the space of an hour. When I asked what she meant, she finally blurted out, "I knew I couldn't have another baby so soon. Not in those circumstances. I didn't think of it as a baby or anything. The abortion hurt a little, but that wasn't any big deal.

When I got home, I picked up Cindy to change her. I looked at her, and I kept seeing this other baby that might have been. That was the only time I felt the immensity of what I had done. I really haven't thought about it much since."

The above stories—all true, but disguised to protect the identities of the individuals, as with all my stories here—show that there are reasons for abortion other than simply backing up failed condoms or skipped pills. Sometimes there are good reasons for an abortion, and you should not have to feel condemned by a society that cannot itself come to a consensus on the subject. One thing you must realize about abortion, though, is that it's *an option only if done early enough.* First you have to figure out how pregnant you are and whether the procedure can be done safely.

To determine just how pregnant you are, you go back to your calendar (now you know why it's so important to keep track of your menstrual cycle) and find out when you last had a period. You pinpoint the first day of that period and count it as Day 1. Then you count the weeks until you arrive at today's date. For example, if your last period was on June 1 and today's date is August 31, you are 13 weeks pregnant. (I know it doesn't make sense, when you probably weren't pregnant on Day 1 of your period, but that is how the doctors figure it, and those are the dates the doctor will be looking at in considering how far along you are for an abortion.)

Unfortunately for many teenagers, denial of the obvious symptoms or sheer ignorance hinder the chances for a safe abortion. The ideal time for an abortion is between 7 and 12 weeks of pregnancy. The type done at this point is called a vacuum suction abortion, and it takes four to seven minutes to perform. For a woman who is less than

12 weeks pregnant, this type of abortion can be done in a clinic relatively easily and safely.

In the book *Changing Bodies, Changing Lives,* Ruth Bell has an excellent chapter on the different methods of abortion and how some people felt who had undergone them. For those of you stricken at the idea of a baby-like fetus swimming around in the aftermath of the suction machine, let me quote the author: "The fetus in most abortions is about the size of a lima bean or a walnut. At three months it is not fully formed and couldn't possibly live outside the mother's womb."

Between 12 and 16 weeks of pregnancy, the D & C (dilation and curettage) abortion is done. General anesthesia is administered, and the doctor may take between twelve and twenty minutes to dilate the cervix and scrape and suction out the contents of the uterus. Naturally it is a more costly and uncomfortable procedure.

A saline abortion is done up to 24 weeks of pregnancy. Briefly, liquid is introduced into the woman's body to start the contractions of labor. This procedure is done in the hospital and involves a two- to three-day stay. It is far more costly, and it is painful. It is also far more traumatic, because the fetus looks more like a baby.

After 24 weeks of pregnancy the fetus is considered viable, and an abortion will not be performed except for a medical emergency. At this stage it would more than likely be a live birth, except for the injection.

If you are thinking of having an abortion, let me advise you that there are two very different types of family planning clinics. Some clinics that advertise free pregnancy testing are really antiabortion organizations that will first show you a graphic film of an abortion. The film usually depicts a late-stage abortion with concomitant trauma to the fetus, which looks very like an infant. It is misleading because first-trimester abortions do not look like that. The film is designed to make you change your mind, to make you decide to continue the pregnancy. These people are not interested in your reasons for having an abortion. They are not concerned with how you're going to afford this baby or whether you are emotionally or physically able to tolerate birth. Antiabortion people have their own agenda, and that is to deter as many people as possible from having abortions.

I'm not suggesting that teenagers seek abortions as a solution to unplanned pregnancies. It is not my intent to teach morality (which is what abortion sometimes comes down to); for some, it is simply the lesser of two evils. I *do* think teenagers ought to be prepared for the kind of deception practiced in some clinics—and it truly is deception practiced on girls at their most vulnerable.

At the other kind of family planning clinic, counselors explain the procedure of abortion and explore your feelings about it—as well as detail the alternatives. It is not their intent to sway you to their way of thinking (whatever that may be)—just to help you make an informed decision. They may show you a film, but it will be of an early abortion and tastefully done—certainly not intended to frighten you.

How do you tell these clinics apart before the damage is done? First, ask others who might have gone to one of them. If that's not possible, choose a clinic but leave at the first indication that the counselor wants to sell you on a certain way of thinking. If you're subjected to a film whose graphic content horrifies you, *get up and leave.* As mentioned earlier, a first-trimester abortion (performed before 12 weeks of pregnancy) will not involve delivery of a baby-like fetus. You'll see blood and tissue.

One thing I learned is that many family planning clinics

that do NOT offer abortions still provide services to a woman who has undergone an abortion elsewhere else. Even if the clinic in your area won't help you get the abortion, once you have gotten it, they may offer you follow-up support (such as a twelve-step recovery program). These programs help the teenager say good-bye to the baby that might have been and to deal with the guilt that comes from having precipitated the baby's loss.

Just because you are young, vulnerable, and asking for assistance shouldn't mean that you give up your ability to choose. It is still a decision that is entirely up to you. Remember, no one has the right to force you to have the baby, or for that matter to have the abortion. Not your counselor, your mother, your doctor, or your boyfriend.

It is hard to avoid having feelings about an abortion— not only because society is in an uproar about women's right to abortion, but because we, as fallible human beings, are likely to make mistakes and blame ourselves for them for an eternity afterward.

You will probably feel angry. About getting into the predicament in the first place. About having to go through this physically when your boyfriend—who had such a great part in the making of the baby—has no immediate sense of the trauma. It's maddening to think back on that moment in time when your boyfriend assured you he'd be there forever and now to realize that *you're* the one having to climb up into the stirrups.

You may be feeling doubly ashamed and guilty. One, for getting pregnant and two, for having an abortion. If you're feeling unsure of your decision, it's important to talk it over with a concerned adult, preferably your parents or a counselor who is sympathetic. Kathy Calder, who heads the Pregnancy and Parenting Project in Augusta, Maine, struck me as unusually sensitive to just this issue.

She told me that her clinic counselors try to explore all possibilities, questioning values to determine whether abortion is a decision the client will be able to look back upon later without undue regret. Abortion is traumatic enough as it is. Don't punish yourself further for having chosen that course.

Guilt comes out in funny ways. Teddie was a junior in high school when she became pregnant. She had been a drug user and had finally come to grips with her addiction. When she had found her way out of the dark and was working on graduating and staying clean, she discovered she was pregnant. In no way was she able to care for a baby, especially a baby conceived during heavy drug use. She talked over her predicament with her school guidance counselor and then went through with an uncomplicated abortion. She seemed to handle the aftermath well, except for one thing. Bad dreams. Dreams about dead babies.

She said, "I dreamed once I had had the baby and was giving it a bath. I left the room for a second—just one second—to get a towel. When I came back, the baby was face down in the tub. Dead. I woke up in a panic, and I remembered that I had killed my baby. It took a while before I realized I hadn't exactly killed it. Not that way."

It is not unusual to have such dreams. What happens is that what you haven't worked through in your mind during the daytime gets tumbled into your dreams at night. Your mind is still trying to work the whole thing out while you sleep. If you have dreams that are repetitive or scary, by all means seek counseling. Chances are that it is *guilt* that is eating at you. Once that is recognized and dealt with, the dreams should stop.

Despite an abortion having been the "right choice," guilt can still plague you for many years. A young woman in her late twenties was once hospitalized under my care because of severe depression and suicidal thoughts. Ellen was a teacher at a prestigious college in Maine. Ten years earlier, while still in high school, she had become pregnant by her boyfriend, Harry. Ellen had plans to go to college the following year; furthermore she was not sure she and Harry could be mates for life. She just wasn't ready for that kind of entanglement. Abortion was legal, so she and Harry drove to Portland to have the abortion. Ellen felt she was making the right decision, but because of her strong religious background she also believed what she was doing was wrong.

She had the abortion, and Harry took her home. Ellen never told her parents or her sisters. She refused to let Harry talk about his own feelings; she just wanted to pretend the whole thing never happened. Later, she kept having bad dreams. She considered talking to her priest, going to confession, but her priest had very strong feelings himself about abortion, and she felt he would merely compound her anguish by censuring her action. Not feeling pardoned, but still feeling guilty, Ellen dropped out of the church. Everytime she saw Harry she remembered the abortion, and in some strange way she started to blame him for the whole thing. They eventually broke up, though they remained friends.

What brought Ellen into the hospital where I worked was the birth of Harry's first child, very near the ten-year anniversary of her abortion. When I saw Ellen, she had tried to overdose on sleeping pills. Her parents had no idea what torment she was going through.

During treatment, in addition to listening to Ellen unload her guilt and anger, I found a sympathetic priest who did not know her. I left them in my office so that Ellen could make a formal confession after all these years, knowing that she would never have to see this priest again. I can't say that the confession alleviated all of Ellen's guilt, but it did help her start talking about the abortion and realize that not all of society condemned her, that even God could forgive her. Gradually she came to see that she had made the right decision at eighteen, even though it was one she wasn't particularly proud of.

It is sad to learn so young that life is not fair. Many of you, unfortunately, have probably already figured that out.

Shrouding the abortion in secrecy (as many teenagers who fear family disapproval feel they must do) only complicates the adjustment afterward. When you can't talk about what you've been through, you can't unburden your guilt or anger or sadness. You can end up feeling like a criminal, bottling up your emotions and denying that anything significant happened. Sometimes women who have had abortions (without supportive counseling) later turn against others who have had the same procedure. Some of the most adamant antiabortion people are those who once had an abortion themselves.

Some girls are just plain scared about abortion. If you're one of them, it's important (for your own peace of mind) to seek as much information as possible about the procedures available. Abortion, if performed early enough, is safer and less painful than a full-term delivery. A good family planning clinic can help you with the specifics. Two good resources for straightforward information are *Changing Bodies, Changing Lives* and *The New Our Bodies, Ourselves.* Most of us (and I certainly include myself) are afraid of things we don't fully understand. Especially our threshold of pain.

I spoke with a young girl who had seen one of the "abortion scare films." Although not considering abortion for herself, she was further frightened about childbirth. "I hadn't really thought about *having* the kid," she said. "But that film made me realize that I was going to have to go through something similar whether I wanted an abortion or a baby. It was scary."

Another feeling common to people who have had abortions is denial, acting as if the whole thing was "no big deal." Ironically, it's as if the woman has no particular feelings at all. If you find yourself not able to conjure up a single feeling, I suggest you dig a little deeper beneath the apathy. Feelings are there, but you may have to search for them. Just because you *think* you don't feel anything about the abortion doesn't mean that you really *don't* feel anything. Some people are able to do something called compartmentalizing the pain. It's as if they can take out the pain and put it in a special drawer and then close the drawer, blocking out the pain. It works for a while, but usually people who block off their pain block off their "good" feelings as well.

More than likely you will have a mixture of the feelings I've described. Perhaps initially you feel relieved that "the problem has gone away." Later you are angry at the world because this happened to you. None of those feelings is wrong.

You are not a bad person because you chose to have an abortion. Abortion is just one alternative that must be examined carefully if you find yourself unexpectedly pregnant. You must feel that it is right for *you*. In my own practice, I have never met anyone who did not express some regret over an abortion. Not that they wouldn't do the same thing all over again. In many cases, given the same circumstances, they would again elect to have the abortion. It's just that they still realize a loss is a loss. It hurts. (See Chapter 9, Lost Babies).

FROM THE MAN'S POINT OF VIEW

What about the guy in all of this? First of all, if the girl decides to have an abortion, there is nothing legally the guy can do to prevent it. Given that, the guy may feel a combination of relief that he doesn't have to worry anymore about the pregnancy and anger at his own powerlessness. (Some guys really want to ground a relationship by having a child. It's also a part of them.) Perhaps they feel a sense of obligation to help the woman through this event. Like some women, they may feel little or nothing. This is called detachment, a way not to have to deal with ambivalent feelings.

Some guys feel nothing but horror about their girlfriend's pregnancy. All they want to do is get as far away from the whole thing as possible. So they run, physically or emotionally, an option not available to the woman carrying the child.

Overall it is more difficult for a guy to feel that initial bonding with the unborn child, because his body is not undergoing the physical changes. I know that some young men grieve the loss of that child, but at this point—in their teen years—they are often not sufficiently invested in either the girlfriend or the pregnancy to grieve for what might have been. For some young men who realize that they have endless years ahead of them in which to start a family, suggesting an abortion to their girlfriend may not seem so horrible a thing.

For those of you who have read this far and decided that abortion is not for you, turn to the next chapter. Short of raising the baby yourself, there is an alternative.

CHAPTER 3

Giving Up the Baby

Adoption agencies are of different types, just as are family planning clinics. At some private religious organizations you can live for the duration of the pregnancy without cost in a home for unwed mothers-to-be. In some private adoption agencies the adoptive couple foot the expenses of your pregnancy and delivery. There are also black market groups that will illegally adopt your baby (with your permission, of course.) In most cases, you will have nothing to do with your child once he or she has been handed over to the adoptive couple. For some of you, that may be just what you want: no further contact. For others, the very fact that you will never see your child grow up may be a deterrent to the whole idea of adoption.

If you are considering adoption (and in Maine only 4 percent of teens choose to give up their babies for adoption, according to 1986 statistics), you can check out your options (either private or through the Department of Health and Human Services) at a family planning clinic. They will explain your choices and refer you to the appropriate agencies. The majority of teens do not consider this alternative, although hundreds of suitable families exist who would love to adopt their child.

Adoption is an alternative to motherhood that was far

more acceptable decades ago. Perhaps because single parenthood has lost much of its stigma, adoption has lost favor in the public eye. Some clinicians feel that there is now greater stigma attached to giving up your baby than to raising the baby as a single parent. All I know is that of the women I've talked with about this issue, most were adamant that they could not have given their child up.

Sharon was a young woman who did choose to give up her baby for adoption. She stayed at a home run by the Catholic Church. She attended the mandatory groups and activities but mostly tried to stay by herself. Sharon's boyfriend was not willing to marry her, and Sharon felt that she would not be able to provide for this baby without family support. Since an older sister had had a baby out of wedlock, Sharon was pretty sure what her family's reaction would be to hers. Her mother would cry and carry on, Sharon reasoned, and remind everyone that she wasn't going to raise another baby herself. Maybe Sharon's mother would tell her to have an abortion. That she would refuse to do; she considered it murder after having seen a television documentary on the subject. Her only alternative, as she saw it, was adoption. Maybe someone else would raise her baby the way she wished she could afford to.

Sharon agonized over her choice. Unlike abortion, where the decision is made and irrevocable once the procedure has taken place, adoption is something you can reconsider all the way up to and past delivery. Sharon tried not to think about the baby growing inside her because it only made her decision to give him up that much harder. She pretended she was at the home because she was ill, an illness that would go away in a few more months.

After the birth, when she had signed away her rights as a parent (as, according to law, her boyfriend also had to do as the baby's father), all she felt was an ugly rage at this boyfriend who had not had to go through this ordeal.

Sharon said, "Jim never felt the baby move. He never stayed awake all night because the baby kept kicking his ribcage. He didn't have to go through anything physical, like I did. It just makes me so mad; it's so unfair. Maybe I'm really mad that I got trapped in this situation, but all I can feel right now is furious that I had to be the only one to suffer. Labor and delivery hurt more than I expected. Maybe if I had had a husband and knew I was going to keep the baby, I wouldn't have minded so much. But I kept reminding myself that the baby wasn't mine and the sooner the ordeal was over, the better."

Many of the women said they tried to feel as little as possible about the pregnancy. They refused to connect to the wonder of pregnancy—the fact that they were carrying a life inside themselves—because that would only have made the impending loss that much greater.

"I didn't want to hear anyone talking about bonding or anything," one said. "I didn't want to feel life because ultimately I knew I'd be giving this child up, and if I didn't notice it in the first place I wouldn't mind so much giving it up."

In these unfortunate circumstances, the woman usually ended up feeling cheated: participating in the miraculous process of birth but getting nothing in the end.

It takes a truly magnanimous person to give up her child because she is concerned for its well-being. When the woman knows she cannot provide for the child and, wanting him or her to have a good chance in life, gives him up for adoption, she ought at least to have the reward of peace of mind. Often, though she may be relieved, there is the ever-present sense of loss.

Like abortion (in which you precipitate the loss) or

miscarriage, adoption also means grieving "the child that might have been." As in any loss, there is denial of pain, anger, a sense of injustice, numbness, and grieving. After all that come eventual acceptance and resignation to the loss. (See Chapter 9, Lost Babies, for further discussion of loss.)

Bonnie, who you'll remember in Chapter 1 chose to get married, told me she never considered adoption because it would have been a "living death." She said, "I couldn't have stood the thought that someone else was raising my kid. What if they weren't nice to her? What if I changed my mind and wanted her back after all this time? What if my own kid hated me for giving her up?"

Melanie chose adoption because, as an abused child herself, she didn't feel her family offered a decent environment for her baby. She stands by her decision to give the baby up, but from time to time she worries and wonders. "Sometimes I wonder," she says, "if his new parents are treating him okay. Sometimes I think if I could only be with him I could keep him safe. But that's kind of stupid, isn't it? I couldn't even keep myself safe!"

Lorna is a woman in her thirties now. When a freshman in college she became pregnant by a guy she had known less than a month, so she chose to drop out of school for a while, have the baby, and give it up for adoption. No one at the school knew except her roommates (and even they didn't know until the moment she dropped out of school). Lorna returned the next semester and went on to finish her education, later becoming a successful lawyer. She says she has no regrets about the adoption, that she no longer wonders if her baby grew up well. Nonetheless, every October 25—the date of his birth—she falls into a mild but inconsolable depression.

If you think adoption might be the best choice for you

and you've looked into the various resources to help you in that decision, be prepared still to feel some sadness. There is just no good way to deal with an unplanned, unwanted pregnancy.

It might be helpful, once you decide on this course of action, to write out a list of reasons why you cannot care for the baby yourself. List also why giving your baby up to another couple would be in the baby's best interests. Keep the list with you, especially at delivery. Then if you choose to hold your baby and get caught up in the emotion of the moment, you can grab your list and remind yourself why keeping the baby just won't work.

Sometimes a woman changes her mind at delivery and keeps the baby, only to discover weeks later that she just cannot care for him, and at that point it is much more painful to give the child up.

Another option is temporary foster care, whereby you give your baby up temporarily to another person's care. When you are in a better position to care for the child yourself, you can regain physical custody. You haven't lost total parental rights, as in adoption.

Foster care is disruptive to both you and the baby. It has its down side and up side, the down being that you miss out on those early opportunities to bond, the up side being that you gain time to mature.

Believe it or not, the baby's father must sign the adoption papers too, waiving his parental rights. I know of one woman who decided to give up her baby only to learn in court that her ex-boyfriend's parents had requested to bring the baby up. The court awarded the baby to them.

I know of few guys (but more guys' mothers) willing to wrest the baby from the mother. Usually the guy will let his girlfriend make that decision for both of them.

Men also do not seem as preoccupied as the women with

looking up their child later. If you think you want to leave the lines open for your child to find you at some point, organizations exist that will assist you in that process. You can place your name in a nationwide file (ask your caseworker) that would allow your child to contact you (should he or she ever decide to look you up in the future). In order to make contact, however, both you and the child would have to request it and make your whereabouts known. You may not want to do this now, but the opportunity exists for the future. Adoption Search Consultants and other similar groups are listed in the Yellow Pages.

Even if you never want to see your grown-up child (and therefore don't intend to make your address available), I urge you NOT to keep that pregnancy a secret from your future spouse (or partner). Occasionally, a child discovers the whereabouts of his biological parents and arrives unannounced on their doorstep, surprising both them and their unsuspecting new families. An unplanned pregnancy may be an unfortunate mistake, but it should never be a "dirty little secret."

The thing to remember about adoption is that it sometimes is a decision that never seems to have an end.

CHAPTER 4

Single Parenthood

Reading this far, you might have the impression that I'm concentrating on the bad things about being pregnant in your teen years. If you're thinking that, wait until you've skimmed this chapter, because if anything is going to sound "bad" it'll be raising the child by yourself.

Don't throw the book on the floor yet. I'm really trying to strike a balance between encouraging you through this "awesome" task and deglamorizing the experience so that others won't follow suit. Of course being a teen parent can be done, and it can be done well too. It's just that raising a baby (married or otherwise) turns out to be more overwhelming than teenagers usually consider.

Let's assume you're pregnant. You aren't in a position to marry, you won't have an abortion, and you can't bear the thought of giving your child up for adoption, even temporarily to foster care. The choice you're left with is to raise the baby yourself. That's a grim prospect for some teenagers, but certainly not for all.

The first feelings of some teenagers are shock and denial. "I can't be pregnant." "This isn't happening to me!" For whatever reasons, the girl ignores the indisputable facts: the missed period, the swollen breasts, the morning nausea, the fatigue, and the mood swings. Either she avoids using a pregnancy test to confirm her suspicions or she simply doesn't consider the possibility of pregnancy at all. I know it is hard to believe that anyone could be pregnant and not realize it, but it happens. Sometimes it's a matter of ignorance: the girl doesn't realize that sex can lead to babies. Sometimes it's more a matter of not *wanting* to know.

Terry was such a girl. Fourteen years old and three months pregnant, she just couldn't believe she was pregnant (even though she was sexually active and using no consistent form of birth control). It was her constant morning nausea that drove her to the doctor, and at twelve weeks of pregnancy she was finally diagnosed. At that point, whether or not she would have chosen an abortion, it was already too late to have a simple one.

The next two cases I'm going to tell you about actually happened within the past two years. Dora was a waitress at a little boardwalk restaurant that catered mostly to tourists. When she returned one summer to start her job, the management noticed that she had gained some weight and waddled when she walked. It wasn't until a tourist from the previous season saw her and exclaimed, "Why, Dora, when are you due?" that the management realized she was pregnant. Dora had not told them because she hadn't realized it herself. A week before her delivery she first saw a doctor and belatedly began prenatal care.

Tonya was caught even more unaware. Growing up in a family of twelve (where her own mother kept having children so often that she could never keep track of them), Tonya escaped everyone's attention. One fall day, she complained of gas pains, went to the bathroom, and delivered a baby boy. She was as shocked as the rest of her family. Fortunately, the baby was later pronounced healthy and sound at the emergency room of the hospital. Tonya had no time to decide ahead how she was going to raise this baby. Nurses later told me that the mother probably incorporated Tonya's baby into her own already overflowing family.

I tell you these stories because denial is so prevalent among teenagers, and because denial is so dangerous. The pregnancy doesn't go away by your ignoring it, but your chances to prepare for it or do something about it *will* go away. With denial, you lose valuable time should you want to terminate the pregnancy. Even if you want to keep the baby, as long as you don't believe you're pregnant you're missing out on valuable prenatal care. Babies can die from lack of proper care and nutrition. During those interminable forty weeks of pregnancy, it's important not only to avoid certain things (drugs, alcohol, and smoking), but also to give your body such things as vitamins and nutritionally balanced meals.

Sometimes young girls are just plain "surprised" by their pregnancy. A recent survey indicates that only 35 percent of teenagers know when the fertile time of their cycle is each month. I asked Jill, a sixteen-year-old mother, if she knew what time of the month she was most likely to get pregnant. She replied, "Let's see, everyone has told me different things. I think it's fourteen days after your period, you can get pregnant. Or maybe it's fourteen days after your period you can't get pregnant. It's one of the two."

Obviously, if you're not sure just when you can get pregnant (and it amounts to four to five days a month), it's imperative to use birth control each and every time you engage in sex. Because how will you know when those four to five days are coming along? Ovulation is often hard to predict. The fourteen-day point is based on a twenty-eight day cycle. Ovulation (barring unforeseen circumstances, such as stress or illness) occurs fourteen days *before the start* of your next period, and you can get pregnant shortly before, during, and shortly after ovulation. (But how do you know ahead of time when your next period will start?) A teenager is too new at the game of predicting menstrual cycles to take chances.

(Actually no one should presume to know her inner workings so well that she takes chances with unprotected sex. My youngest child is the result of that kind of smug thinking.)

Sometimes the surprise takes a different twist. Karen was using the pill faithfully, though it didn't agree with her and she was constantly throwing up. Her doctor told her to stay with it a while longer and give her system a chance to get used to the extra hormones. What he neglected to tell her was to use some other form of birth control additionally until the vomiting stopped. Karen got pregnant, taking the pill every night.

Fanny was another girl intelligent in all matters except the heart. She never considered using birth control regularly, although she had taken a sex education course (even got an A in it) and knew (on one level) that it was possible to get pregnant with *just one* unprotected act of sex. Unfortunately, she didn't think it would happen to *her*. She got pregnant at sixteen.

Sex education classes seem to be making an impression on high school teenagers; in my own community the number of pregnant girls has dropped recently. However, the alarming news is an increase in the number of pregnant twelve- and thirteen-year-olds. These are the kids who believe an assortment of myths: "If I do it less than five times, I won't get pregnant." "If I stand up right after sex, I won't get pregnant." "If I do it during my period, I won't get pregnant."

The truth is that you can get pregnant at age twelve for the same reason you can get pregnant at age seventeen or age thirty. Any act of unprotected sex *can* lead to pregnancy if it's the right time of the month. Jumping up afterward and running around the room to let the semen leak out will do little more than get you out of breath and sticky.

As with anything else, teenagers are often angry when they realize they're pregnant. Angry that they're in this predicament—having to make a decision, angry at the loss of control over their lives and the uncertain future.

Karen, the girl who had responsibly used the pill for birth control, found herself pregnant at the start of her senior year. A good athlete, she was looking forward to being captain of some of the teams. All that changed when she became pregnant; obviously she couldn't waddle down center court or run hurdles carrying thirty extra pounds.

"I missed out on that year, and though I'm happy with my daughter now," she told me, "I'll never get that year back."

Other girls, perhaps better grounded in reality or simply pessimistic, get bogged down worrying over how they will support a baby. Or survive labor and the physical uncertainties of pregnancy. (See Chapter 8, Physical and Emotional Reality, for a more complete discussion.)

For those of you who haven't a boyfriend or family to rely on for support, there are nurses and social workers who can work with you, as well as public assistance available for prenatal care, housing, and counseling. Check with your community family planning clinic. People there should be able to link you with a public health nurse and other agency resources. Don't waste time worrying. There is help out there, but you have to ask for it.

Along with anger and fear, some girls feel regret early on in their pregnancy. Sometimes a girl really wants to get pregnant—more or less to see if she has the ability to conceive. Then when she has conceived, she panics and thinks, "Oh, no, what have I done?" She realizes at this point that she won't be buying that dress for the spring prom. She won't be playing Juliet in the senior play when she's two weeks short of delivery. It's kind of like seeing your life pass before your eyes, only (I'm told) in this case it's all the missed opportunities that rush past, not the memories.

Not everyone is "felled" by pregnancy, as unanticipated as the event may be. Some girls told me they were thrilled when they realized they were pregnant. It was an accomplishment; it marked their emergence into adulthood. These girls usually had easy, nausea-free pregnancies, and they felt their "glow" throughout the long nine months. It was something they either wanted or welcomed.

Sometimes the good feelings are based on the assumption that the unborn baby will give you unconditional love. Actually textbooks will tell you that only parents and dogs can give "unconditional" love—or love that is given no matter what comes back in return. (Note that I said *can* give, not *give*. That's because not all parents are capable themselves of giving unconditional love.) But a baby will not fulfill your wish to be loved. That baby is not asking to come into this world. And he has the opposite idea anyway: that *you're* there to fulfill *his* need to be loved and cared for. It's not until they're much older—maybe three or four—that you'll see them try to give you something back. Some babies won't even smile when you burp them. Talk about ingratitude!

Randi was fifteen when she discovered she was pregnant. She was thrilled, even though she knew she would be raising the baby herself. Her boyfriend had gone off and joined the Air Force before the pregnancy test turned up positive. Randi's father had left the family when she was two. Her mother had died when Randi was ten, and now Randi lived alternately with an older brother and an older married sister. To Randi, it always seemed that everyone left her or pushed her away. Now that she was pregnant, she reasoned, she'd have someone—the baby—who would always be there, always be hers.

Shawna was another girl who always felt a little out of step with kids at school. She was scared of the "popular" girls because she didn't think she measured up to them. She didn't have their money or nice clothes, and she wasn't especially pretty. But when she became pregnant that no longer mattered. She felt special because she was doing something grown-up, something that meant someone had found her desirable. She told me about the time she'd been walking downtown and spotted a group of the popular girls hanging out in front of the drugstore.

Shawna said, "Before, I would have been too scared to walk past them. I would have figured they were all watching me, making fun of my clothes or the way I walked. This time I didn't care. I sailed right on by them. I even said hi. I just wanted to shout, 'Hey, look at me. I'm going to be a mother. So who cares what I'm wearing.' It was a great feeling. I felt powerful, having made a baby and all."

At the other end of the spectrum, you may be feeling embarrassed over your blossoming pregnancy. Though people of my generation seemed to have more hang-ups—more things that caused us to squirm with embarrassment—teenagers nowadays may still be uncomfortable with their condition, especially if they continue to go to school. There's nothing like asking permission to go to the bathroom three times in one class or sitting two feet away from the desk because you're too pregnant to get any closer. In those cases, you might be feeling happy about the pregnancy, but your dignity got left behind along the way.

Not surprisingly, pregnant teenagers can get depressed too. Not all of them, but some do when they contemplate the turn their life has started to take. Depression (feeling down, blue, sad) is merely anger turned on yourself. It encompasses hopelessness, futility, and at the extreme end, thoughts of suicide. "What am I going to do? I can't have this baby. My Dad will kill me if he finds out."

Periods of depression are not uncommon for a girl suddenly facing an unplanned pregnancy. The pregnancy itself can account for some of the "down" times, because your hormones are all out of whack. It's okay to be discouraged, sad, or blue; it's even normal. What isn't okay is when your feelings don't lift or your thoughts become serious plans to hurt yourself. Suicidal thoughts, even if you don't have a concrete plan of action, need immediate attention by a trained professional. Call the suicide hotline, a counseling agency, your minister, the hospital, or the police. Don't feel you have to go through this alone, and don't feel it's a sign of character to weather by yourself every crisis that comes along. I have always told my clients that it's a sign of strength to know when you need to ask for help. Your life is out of control right now, and it's hard to make any decision, let alone the right one. Don't be afraid to seek out a concerned adult.

FROM THE MAN'S POINT OF VIEW

I haven't forgotten you men. Although your girlfriend may opt to have this baby herself, you certainly still have feelings about the whole thing. Some guys are relieved that they're not going to be pushed into a marriage they don't want. They (erroneously) believe their responsibilities ended when their girl got pregnant. If you're one of them—relieved not to have to concern yourself anymore with the pregnancy or child—you are in for a rude surprise. *Your responsibility does not end.* In fact, it won't end for at least another eighteen years.

You, as the father, are responsible for child support until the child is eighteen years old. Even if you are not married to the child's mother, even if it was only a one-night stand, *you are still responsible.* If the child's mother applies for government assistance (AFDC), she may not get it unless she names you as the father. Then the government is entitled to take part of your wages for child support. So while you may be relieved that you won't be involved in the day-to-day care and raising of the baby, realize that you must still support him or her.

You may be confused when your girlfriend tells you she's pregnant. "What am I supposed to do now?" Rich is one who first felt that way. He had know Mia only a few months and had dated her for two weeks before discovering that they had little in common. In fact, he didn't even like her very much. Several weeks after they broke up, Mia caught up with him in the hall running to class.

"I'm pregnant," she told him. "What are you going to do about it?"

Rich was shocked. He knew there was good reason for her to be pregnant by him, but he couldn't believe it was happening because he didn't like her anymore.

Rich suggested an abortion. Mia wouldn't hear of it. Rich explained that he had no intention of marrying her, so Mia said, "I'll raise the baby myself then."

Mia was immediately kicked out of her home. Rich,

feeling responsible (especially when he discovered she was only fifteen, not seventeen as she had claimed), invited her to move in with his family.

When I asked why he had done that, he said, "It wasn't because I loved her and wanted to marry her later. It just was the *right* thing to do, that's all. I knew right from wrong, and I needed to take care of her." Nonetheless, he is still not certain what that entails, how much he should be involved.

Some guys feel proud that they've fathered a child. Max was like that. He was ten years older than his girlfriend, who was fourteen at the time of her pregnancy. Max thought it was great that she was pregnant. He had no concept of what parenthood required; his contribution was to buy diapers for the baby once a week after it was born.

Some guys may be angry. Maybe the anger focuses on the girl who is carrying their baby. Maybe on the government for making him support a child he never wanted.

Hank was a high school sophomore when his girlfriend got pregnant. Neither cared enough about the other to marry, but Hank still wanted to be involved in their baby's welfare. During his senior year he rearranged his class schedule so that he could baby-sit while his ex-girlfriend went to classes. After graduation his ex-girlfriend gave him custody of their child. Hank, although with good intent, just couldn't manage single parenthood and work. His mother ended up raising the baby, and Hank grew increasingly depressed at his early failure to be a good father.

Some guys feel no responsibility toward the child or the child's mother. Ted told me during therapy, "I gave Lisa some money toward an abortion, but she didn't get one. I can't help that. I told her I didn't want to be involved; I didn't want that kid. My part is finished; I don't intend to spend the rest of my life supporting a kid I didn't want in the first place. She wanted it; let her raise it."

Although Ted claimed that he felt no responsibility toward the baby or its mother, he was so angry that it wasn't hard to pick up on his ambivalence. It was several months before he could admit his own anger and tie it into his need to see himself as a good person, one who doesn't turn his back on others. Ted did end up sending money to Lisa for child support, although he still wrestled with the role of "father."

I have yet to see many guys who are enthusiastic about their young girlfriend's pregnancy, especially when they don't plan to marry. However, some guys are still interested and committed, despite initial shock and anger. I've talked with some girls and their boyfriends who do their weekly grocery shopping together, although the girl still lives with her parents and raises the baby with their support. The men all seem genuinely interested in their children and remain involved, even though their own relationship with the baby's mother appears shaky.

Single parenthood doesn't have to be the end of the world. It *is* hard: after all, without a partner you have to shoulder twice the responsibilities. You have twice the chores and only half the support, but with community and family help single parenthood can be made easier.

In the next section, I shall examine how your pregnancy affects the rest of your life: school, friends, and family. Then I'll look at the physical and emotional reality of the pregnancy: how you might feel as the pregnancy progresses. It's going to be a long road...

P A R T ◇ II

ADJUSTMENTS DURING PREGNANCY

CHAPTER ◇ 5

Your Education

I n this chapter, I shall explore how your pregnancy affects the other parts of your life. One of the biggest traps for pregnant teens is choosing not to complete their schooling. I realize that not everyone is cut out for college, but for that matter, not everyone *needs* a college degree. A high school diploma is different. The sad thing that often happens when a teenager becomes pregnant is that she drops out of school. Or her boyfriend, realizing that he will need to support a child, drops out to take on an additional job.

Scrambling to find ways to cover the bills is an awful way to live. Without a high school diploma, you subject yourself to minimum-wage jobs for the rest of your life. Money will be a constant concern, as if the new problems of parenthood will not be troubling enough. However you do it, I hope you complete high school because (as an adult who herself has seen financially troubling times) I know that getting a good job, feeling good about yourself because you can support your family, is one of the most important things you can do in your life.

Of course, it's hard to stay in school. First of all, you're probably too embarrassed to attend classes right through your pregnancy. Bonnie told me about feeling embarrassed. When she was first pregnant, she still rode the bus to school, hoping to go on with her education as if nothing had changed. The problem was that she was different now, and one of the biggest lessons I learned in my adolescence was that *no one wants to be different.* Bonnie not only was married, she was pregnant. And visibly so. Some kids tittered behind her back because she looked funny waddling down the aisle of the bus, then trying to squeeze herself into a seat. Some might have tittered because they were uncomfortable with the idea of Bonnie's sexuality. (That can make a person nervous if he or she is embarrassed about the whole idea of sex.) But whatever the reasons for other people's behavior, it doesn't make it any easier to parade your body around the schoolyard, which is exactly what Bonnie felt she was doing. Bonnie finally dropped out of school to have the baby. Ten years later she is now back in a program to earn her high school diploma.

"So I can start feeling good about myself," she told me. "I always believed I wasn't as good as anyone else because I hadn't finished high school."

Aside from looking different, you'll probably be acting different too. Morning sickness and school don't mix well. Who wants to keep running back and forth to the restroom all day?

Sometimes it's not even a matter of embarrassment about your appearance. When a woman is pregnant, it's normal for her to be consumed with what is going on inside her. She fantasizes about the unborn child, she names it, she wonders what it'll be like to cuddle this new life squirming around inside right now. Much of her energy is spent just thinking about the baby. The same is true of a teenager. She is preoccupied with the "miracle of life" unfolding inside her. Will she have a baby shower? Will she do okay in labor and delivery? Will she be a good mother? Will her baby love her? What will it look like? With all this wondering and figuring, it's not hard to see that there's little room for studying.

Some girls aspire to nothing beyond motherhood. "I'm not the type of girl who wants a career," Nicole told me. "I'm going to stay home and take care of my family, so what does it matter if I drop out of school a little early?"

Well, I'm certainly not going to argue with your desire to stay home with the baby instead of cultivating a career. After all, I've done both. The thing about dropping out of school is that you limit your chances for the future by deciding at age fifteen or sixteen that you will never want a career. What if your boyfriend doesn't come through with the money? What if your soon-to-be husband discovers that he hates being married and wants a divorce? What if your parents tell you you're on your own now? I don't know what is your concept of welfare assistance, but let me assure you, it's never enough. With no money and no job prospects (beyond those that will give you only a bare subsistence), you will be trapped in that house, bound to your young children, and eventually resentful of your loss of a meaningful life.

There have been times when I stayed home to raise my three children. The difference for me—in the past, a career woman—was that I knew I had the means by which to secure a well-paying job if I needed it. I always knew I could take care of myself, and I think that's important in feeling good about yourself.

If you teenagers are anything like me twenty years ago, you're probably reading this chapter with about as much gusto as you'd feel preparing for midterms. When I was in college, all I wanted to do was get married; I was afraid the opportunity would pass me by and I'd never get another. I figured I could interrupt my college career, get married, and work at any old job to help keep my husband in school. Then we'd raise a family, and I'd eventually get around to finishing college—though I don't know what I intended to do with the kids in the meantime.

Fortunately for me, my father talked me out of it. He predicted that I'd never finish my education if I turned my back on it right then. I thought at the time that he was condemning me to the single life forever because by the time I finished school (to his satisfaction) I'd be too old to arouse *anyone's* interest in marriage.

When I was going to graduate school (and was also married), I realized what a hard task I had set for myself. Looking back at my plan to abandon school for marriage, I realized I probably never would have made my way back into the system. The longer you're out, the harder it is.

Sometimes (and this was true for some of the women I interviewed for this book) the girl has already given up on school and dropped out. Then she gets pregnant, almost as if (though I'm not saying this is the case) the pregnancy comes along to give her something to do. Terry, at fourteen, had been fed up with school. Like so many other teenagers, she didn't abruptly decide to quit; it happened gradually. She missed a few days, she attended on others, then skipped a week or so. The overburdened guidance department gave up tracking down teenagers who couldn't make up their minds to remain students. Terry admits she just "fazed out" of school, and no one came after her to make her return.

I don't pretend to know why all teenagers drop out of school. Obviously Terry and girls like her had found little academic success in the past. For a pregnant teenager already in academic difficulty, pregnancy often is the best reason (in her eyes) to drop out of school. "Why bother now?" she seems to say.

SPECIAL PROGRAMS

Okay. So much for regular classes. But that is not the only way to get an education or a diploma. Several special programs are in operation to help the pregnant teenager fulfill her school obligations and raise her child as well. Some places have "mentor programs" whereby an older teen or adult is paired with a newly pregnant teenager. This older teen helps the younger one navigate the difficulties in getting assistance and may even act as a tutor.

Other schools encourage the girl to graduate by attending adult education classes, so that she no longer has to attend school with people her own age who might make her feel uncomfortable.

Special programs linked with the school (or adult education) serve as an alternative to regular classes. In one program I visited, the girls (most of whom had children and could bring them for day-care in the same building) attended classes with other kids in similar circumstances. Because the building was not on school grounds, the girls did not feel conspicuous for attending something *different*—hence, inferior. It simply was a different program to fulfill different needs. The girls learned at their own pace, received a lot of individual attention, and more important, had the opportunity to discuss (in a class setting with professionals) what was happening in their lives now that they had had children or were in the process of having them.

Other school programs, equally successful, blend students into the mainstream of regular classes. The teenagers in one of these programs did not feel awkward around the other nonpregnant students. Baby-sitters at the parenting center (located right on campus) looked after their babies, and the only difference between these girls and their peers was that they arrived at school and departed with infants. They were thus able to attend classes (without having to worry about who would care for their baby and at what cost) and finish their high school education. The staff of this innovative program supported the girls and gave them something more to aspire to than a minimum-wage job and child-care hassles.

Some of these programs encourage teen fathers to participate as well. Guys, especially ones who opt to help support their new family, often feel stretched thin through the demands of work, homework, and thoughts of impending fatherhood. They have little energy left to concentrate on studies, perhaps fearing they may eventually have to give up their aspirations for further schooling. Programs such as the one mentioned earlier can offer supportive counseling to the troubled teen father. These programs are popping up all over the country because of the large number of pregnant teenagers. I guess lawmakers have decided that if they can't prevent teenage pregnancies, they should do something to help the pregnant teen finish her schooling (with the idea of stemming the tide of government-assisted, undereducated teen parents.)

No matter today that you're embarrassed or uncomfortable about being pregnant and in school, you can search out alternatives to strike a balance between your needs for privacy and for an education. Your diploma (and certainly college) is your opportunity to break out of the cycle of poverty and low self-esteem.

CHAPTER 6

Friends

W hen I was fresh out of school, I went to work at a psychiatric hospital, where I made friends with a woman my age who worked in another department. I think I liked Pat so much because she was so much like me. Everytime I had a problem, she had either just gone through something similar or was in the middle of the same thing. Pat and I married similar men during the same summer, and both our first husbands turned out to be the irresponsible jerks others had warned us they would be. We agonized over our marriages and whether or not we should end them. And these experiences actually weren't so bad because we had each other with whom to share them.

One day Pat was sick at work. For the next couple of weeks she continued to get sick, only in the mornings. I should have guessed she was pregnant, but I just figured she would have told me if she were. A month later Pat admitted she was pregnant. I was stunned because I had assumed that was something we would do at the same time. I watched Pat go through her pregnancy, but I never felt involved. I didn't understand her moods or her nesting instinct—wanting to stay home and create a place for the baby. If her husband was still a jerk, she didn't tell me; she was all wrapped up in the coming baby. I'll admit that I was jealous. Jealous of this baby who had come between us and angry that Pat had interests other than I had.

After Pat had her little girl, I visited once or twice, but I felt clumsy and awkward around the baby. Pat had changed overnight into this new creature—a mother, and I didn't know how to relate to her. Pat was preoccupied with her kid's bowel movements and weight gains, and I was in the throes of a divorce. I wasn't getting sympathy or advice from Pat. I thought she had suddenly lost her mind and turned into this mush of a person whose only interest was a kid who cried all the time and spit up everytime you picked her up. Pat seemed fascinated with her; she couldn't wait to tell me when her daughter first rolled over, but I tell you, that held about as much joy for me as watching a ball game go ten extra innings.

Years later when I had my own first child, I couldn't stop marveling just as Pat had done. I was sure my daughter smiled at me at three days old, and I carried her with me everywhere. I was convinced that everyone in the world wanted to know Michal's latest doings, and if they didn't I told them anyway. One night I remembered my friend Pat, who had since moved away. I wanted so much to call her up and say, "I understand now. I understand."

Many things can change your relationship with your best friend over the years: One of you marries, one moves away, one has a baby. Even though babies are supposed to be cute little bundles, it's hard to believe they can alter your friendships as much as they do.

When you're pregnant you may find it hard to relate to your friends who aren't married and aren't pregnant. You have different interests, and it will take a lot of effort to understand each other's life right now.

Aside from the glow of accomplishment, you may feel regret. You won't be attending the senior prom this year, and you can't "party" anymore—not if you're concerned about your baby's well-being. Drugs, alcohol, and babies don't mix. If you want a healthy baby, you'll have to stay far away from those things and the friends who still pursue them.

Chandra told me that her best friend was angry with her now that Chandra had a baby. I asked if it were because Chandra had something she didn't have, but Chandra thought it was because her friend didn't like to party without her. She felt that Chandra had deserted her.

Right after the birth, Chandra was so excited about the baby that she didn't mind staying home night after night. Soon, though, the novelty of looking after a baby who cried all the time wore off, and Chandra grew resentful of her best friend's freedom.

Ironically, the best friend who thought Chandra was crazy for giving up her freedom (both girls were fourteen) became pregnant shortly after Chandra's baby was a month old. Now Chandra is looking forward to her best friend's once again having things in common with her. The sad part is that I think the two girls have the fantasy that they'll get a sitter for their babies and go partying together at night. Like old times . . .

It's frustrating for everyone concerned when someone in your group gets pregnant. The other girls become bored hearing about your pregnancy once the newness wears off, and you probably tire of hearing about events you can no longer participate in. Differences sometimes complicate relationships, particularly if the two or three of you can't talk about the subject and find some middle ground.

Years ago I ran a group for inpatients at the hospital where I worked. One girl who had a baby thought the world existed just to ponder her postpartum depression. Finally a woman in the group jumped up one day and shouted, "If you say one more word about your baby or your hard life, I'm going to throw up. I've heard enough to last me a lifetime."

To a certain extent you may find yourself in the same boat with your friends, who aren't interested in hearing about your baby because *they aren't having a baby too.*

If drugs and alcohol are part of your friendships, you'll have to find some new friends or pressure your friends to give up their vices around you. In the first three months of pregnancy, drugs—even some prescription drugs—can damage the fetus's development. Remember, whatever you—the mother—ingest crosses the placental barrier, and the baby ingests it too. Beer and wine coolers that can supposedly make you relax can retard the baby's growth and in severe cases cause the baby's death. There is no time when a pregnant woman can safely drink alcohol. Believe that. In the end your friends may not appreciate your new circumstances causing them to change their habits.

Some girls tell me that at least one friend tries to maintain the old ties. They say that they both make extra efforts to keep the friendship going, but invariably they add, "It's not the same, though."

So how do you cope with the havoc your pregnancy wreaks on your friendships? First of all, you have to accept that your friends won't always change just because you did, and they probably won't marvel at your new situation if it's nothing they want themselves at this time. You can keep these people in your life, but as the pregnancy progresses I suspect they will take a back seat to other acquaintances.

You might consider a whole new set of friends that reinforce a positive image and have more in common with you.

I can hear you fuming, "Well, where do I find these people?"

It's not hard. There are special classes and support groups for pregnant teenagers still in school. (You read about some in the last chapter.) Some are associated with the school, and others are affiliated with the YWCA. You are not the only pregnant teenager in your community who needs these services. You should be able to find others who have either been where you are now or are going through it too. Called peer support groups, these groups are popping up all over the country to serve the needs of pregnant teenagers. It's just a matter of asking where they are in your community.

Then, too, when you take Lamaze classes, you will meet an assortment of people preparing for birth. I've been through these childbirth classes, and they are a wonderful way to learn about delivery and pregnancy and make friends too. When I took the classes, we were all as interested in hearing about each other's aches and pains as we were in the deliveries. I felt I had a whole group of people cheering me on as I weathered the stages of pregnancy.

(By the way, in taking Lamaze classes you don't necessarily commit yourself to an unmedicated childbirth. The classes merely help you understand the process. You can still ask for medication for your delivery.)

Last of all, don't lose sight of the fact that you have a life beyond that of being a mother. You will get tired of tying yourself down to your baby. Cultivate other interests by hanging onto some of your old friends and letting them keep you involved in the world at large. You may not feel as close to them as you once did, but you don't have to go to the other extreme of shutting them out of your life. Your life shouldn't come to a standstill simply because you've become a mother. Keep involved, keep challenged so that you feel alive and important. Your baby will eventually grow up and leave your home. What you have done with your life up to that point will sustain you once the kids have left the nest.

Again, I haven't forgotten the men in this chapter. Depending on how involved they are with their girlfriend/ wife, they will face some of the same problems. They, too, may see less and less of their old friends, particularly those who use drugs and drink. Some guys can adapt better than others. Some will be angry that their girlfriend/wife requires them to give up some of their pastimes (even self-destructive ones.) Perhaps they feel they've given up enough.

Those of you who spend less time with your hard-drinking buddies may find yourself resentful, not only because you've had to change, but also because your girlfriend may not be able to fill the gap left by these friends. She may be preoccupied with the coming baby, which leaves you feeling even more jealous and deserted.

For you, I'd also suggest getting involved with other guys in the same circumstances, or joining your girlfriend in Lamaze classes—for the knowledge as well as the peer support. Cultivating new friends doesn't have to mean discarding all the old ones. Like your girlfriend, you still need contact with others who are involved in different pursuits.

I guess to sum up this chapter I'd say it's about how your friendships usually change when you're pregnant; that it's neither good nor bad that they change; and that it sometimes helps to find a new circle of friends with similar interests while hanging onto old friends so that your life won't revolve simply around pregnancy and babies. Some day your old friends may have similar concerns, and they may look *you* up as the authority on the subject.

You don't have to close doors to open new ones.

CHAPTER ◇ 7

Family

For many teenagers I spoke with, the hardest thing they had to do was tell their parents they were pregnant. Some girls went to great lengths to avoid having to tell them. In this chapter I will tell you stories of families pulling together to give the teenager as much support as she or he needs to weather the difficulties of teenage pregnancy. I'll also tell you stories of just the opposite—families who turned their backs on the teenagers out of anger, shame, or ignorance.

Your relationship with your parents before your pregnancy will determine to a large extent the ease with which you tell your earthshaking news now. In an already overburdened family, your parents may not react to the pregnancy beyond sighing that they figured you'd wind up pregnant. In other cases—even worse—your parents may not be in good enough emotional shape themselves to provide you with any kind of support or advice. One girl told me that when she confessed to her mother she was three months pregnant, her mother fell apart, screaming and carrying on about her daughter's ruined life. Pamela ended up consoling her mother, telling her that things wouldn't be so bad, that she'd manage somehow. She then went on to list the agencies that would probably help with finances, and eventually her mother calmed down. Years later Pamela still recalled having to console her mother at a time in her life when she felt *she* was the one needing support.

Some of you may be anxious that the news of your pregnancy will send your parents into orbit: a disappointment so monumental that they'll never get over it. Your parents may initially respond badly, but that doesn't mean they won't eventually stand by you. (Sometimes it wasn't until the baby was born that the parents accepted the situation.)

Many of the girls I interviewed said they thought their parents—especially their father—would "kill them." It's probably hard to believe that some parents react so badly simply because they care so much for you. I guess they have an exalted idea that they can give you the world and keep you safe from hardship at the same time. Discovering that you've gone out and created circumstances guaranteed to complicate your young life is no doubt more of a shock than they can initially absorb. Remember, they may be just as mad at themselves for not protecting you as they are at you for getting in this predicament. You just have to get past everyone's initial hysteria.

Sometimes teenagers interpret their parents' strong reactions as shame and disgust. Then they absorb those very feelings, ending up feeling as guilty as they believe their parents consider them. A teenage pregnancy is indeed a family crisis, but it doesn't have to be the family's undoing. Often members pull together, despite their feelings of morality, for the very reason that they *do* love you.

One girl told me she felt too embarrassed to tell her parents she was pregnant. Lucy came from a religious family of upper middle-class background. She had always been an excellent student, serious enough about her studies to plan to go to an Ivy League college. In her senior year in high school, she became involved with a guy at school. He was good-looking and charismatic, and before she knew it she was sexually involved with him. She kept this aspect of their relationship from her parents, but after every date with Peter she felt horribly guilty. She would tiptoe past her parents' bedroom and pray they wouldn't awaken and come to talk with her. She was sure they would sense immediately that she had had sex with Peter, and she knew they considered sex before marriage as morally reprehensible and nothing their daughter would do. When Lucy ended up pregnant, she was mostly ashamed because now they would know about her and Peter. She felt terrible about having let them down, not to mention afraid of the consequences to the rest of her life.

Many girls said they were relieved when they finally told their parents. "It was all out in the open: I didn't have to lie awake at night anymore wondering how they would take the news," Susan, age sixteen, told me. "There was a lot of shouting and cursing at first, but we all survived it. Now my mother even takes me shopping for maternity clothes."

Allison was another girl who was afraid to tell her mother she thought she was pregnant. "There had been one family crisis after another that spring. I wasn't thrilled about dropping another bomb on her right then, but I told her anyway. You know what? She was just great. She told me I needed to get checked by our family doctor, and she even went with me for the appointment. I was actually relieved that when the doctor gave me the verdict my mother already knew. She had had to get married herself, so I guess she didn't think she had the right to go crazy when I did the same thing."

To portray only closely knit families responding in a supportive fashion would be to ignore the many other families who don't behave that way. Some families are so torn apart by constant turmoil that they have no energy left to deal with one more crisis. Sometimes the parents are divorced and they turn on each other, accusing each other of failing to bring up the girl or boy properly. That, of course, isn't the point. You know yourself that you don't need your parents arguing over whose fault it was that you got pregnant. That just puts you in the middle of another battle, and it does nothing to solve the problem at hand. If your parents have always responded to a personal crisis by attacking each other or falling apart, maybe you should enlist the support of another adult in breaking the news to them—a counselor, a doctor, a social worker.

As long as we're on the subject, let's look at how you go about telling your parents in the first place. Part of the problem may be the circumstances in which you choose to break the news. If you're coming in late from a date, and your father is standing there on the front porch fuming about your total disregard for parental wishes, shouting back that you're also three months pregnant isn't going to put things in a better light. That would be like throwing gasoline on a fire.

Instead, choose a time when your parents seem relaxed. Perhaps after the dinner dishes are done or are sloshing away in the dishwasher. Perhaps after your Dad has watched the evening news (everything pales in comparison to the evening news).

Practice ahead of time what you want to say. You don't have to anticipate your parents' every reaction; you just need to know what you want to say *first*. There's nothing worse than getting their attention and then not knowing what to do with it. Sometimes my middle daughter wanders into the kitchen with a hangdog look, and I know she wants to tell me she's done something wrong. But half the time, anticipating my anger, she hesitates before launching into her spiel and ends up saying, "Oh, forget it."

"Well, what did you want to tell me?" I prod.

"Oh, nothing," she says, which drives me crazier than I would have been in the first place. At that point I not only have to hear the bad news, I have to drag it out of her as well.

If you think your parents will react badly, it's helpful to know a little of what you plan to do in the near future, so you can tell them that too. Knowing that you're not falling apart yourself might encourage them to view the whole thing less negatively.

Realize, too, that even if your parents "go crazy" when they first hear the news, chances are they will calm down and handle it better once they've gotten over the initial shock. I've always marveled at how my own mother could fall apart when I dropped some unwelcome piece of news on her, but by the time she told Dad about it she had recovered enough to keep him from coming unglued. Believe it or not, parents are human too. They won't always take news of their teenager's pregnancy in a calm, welcoming manner, but they can come around, especially when they realize that they're needed.

In cases where the pregnancy is a result of incest, I wouldn't suggest treating the matter as simply as I have described. In such a potentially explosive situation I would urge you to have an adult you trust at hand to keep the situation from disintegrating into an ugly mess. The pregnancy may be a catalyst for your mother (or parents, depending on who is involved) to seek action against the perpetrator of the sexual abuse. Whatever the circumstances, you shouldn't go through it alone.

* * *

Okay, at this point you have determined that you're pregnant and have told your parents. What happens next?

Well, as I said, I can't guarantee that everyone's parents
will come through for them. But I can assure you that *if*
your parents support you, you should have an easier time.

My colleagues tell me that parents don't always respond
admirably. Some girls they've seen in counseling were
actually kicked out because they had become pregnant.
Perhaps their behavior had continually taxed their parents,
but whatever the reasons, they were out on their own,
without shelter or resources, and seven months or so shy of
having a baby to support.

Mia had that unfortunate experience. She became pregnant at fifteen, and her mother (her parents were divorced)
told her to leave, that she'd have to fend for herself. Mia
moved in with some school friends, but they soon tired of
her moodiness and her disregard for house rules. Friends
kept asking Mia to leave until she had finally exhausted all
her contacts. She eventually wound up living with her
ex-boyfriend's family, though she felt certain they were
only helping her in order to find evidence that she was an
unfit mother. Her mother never relented and let her come
home. Today Mia has dropped out of school; she
periodically finds stable living conditions so that the welfare department has no grounds to take her child away. It's
a constant battle, and she looks much older than sixteen
now.

A colleague told me about another case with a more
positive ending. Jainey was also kicked out of her home by
more middle-class parents who disapproved not only of her
boyfriend but also her decision to keep the baby. They said
she could stay if she agreed to an abortion. When Jainey
refused, they told her to pack her bags. Jainey too turned

to her friends, who took her in at first. Later Jainey made her way to a woman's resource center, and they helped her find a place to live and money with which to finance prenatal care and eventually child care. Jainey finished high school with their help. Not only that, she finished college five years later and had sufficiently impressed her parents so that they were in the audience at graduation, applauding like crazy.

As you can see, while getting cut off from family support makes it harder for the adolescent, it just means that she has to turn elsewhere for emotional and financial support. The Department of Health and Human Services can help. Peer support groups can provide emotional support; YWCAs sometimes house pregnant teenagers who are homeless. Family planning clinics understand that pregnant teenagers don't always have the support of their parents. The clinics know of resources to help with shelter, prenatal care, and schooling. You don't have to give your baby up for adoption or have an abortion to be eligible for help.

On the negative side, families sometimes try to force teenagers into having an abortion. Remember: *No one can force you to have an abortion.* Instead of simply cutting your ties to your parents under these circumstances, you might first listen to their reasons for suggesting such a course of action. Perhaps they can explain in a helpful way why they feel the way they do. Perhaps you too, in a less heated exchange, can explain your own feelings.

But if the two or three of you can't come to any agreement, perhaps it is better to seek outside intervention to enable you to support yourself without succumbing to their wishes and then hating them for it.

Some girls are too young to resist their parent's wishes, and I'm not suggesting that in some circumstances the parents don't want the best for their children. Nonetheless, if things are done against your wishes, you aren't likely to forgive or forget it anytime soon. A nurse at a local hospital told me of a case in which the parents of a teenager in labor decided that their daughter should give her baby up for adoption. The nurse had no argument with the plan; after all, the girl was only thirteen, a veritable child herself. However, the nurses had been instructed to whisk the newborn infant away before the girl could see it and change her mind. The nurses felt cruel, taking the baby away from the girl, who acted as if she had no say in the matter.

Some families, while offering support and shelter for the single mother, send mixed messages at the same time. Gail, age sixteen, told me that her parents had been great, even fixing up a room for the coming infant. But her brothers missed no chance to shame her about her pregnancy. Her older brother said to her one night, "So that's what you've been doing with Jack in your spare time."

One woman I heard of had a daughter who had moved out to live with her boyfriend against her parents' wishes. Learning that Linda was pregnant, Sally drove to the next town to talk to her daughter. She offered to let Linda come back home to receive prenatal care and emotional support. Linda agreed, especially since her boyfriend had recently abandoned her. While she may not have felt she was returning home under the best of circumstances, she was relieved not to have to worry about health care during her pregnancy or where she would live once the baby was born. Sally hadn't approved of what Linda did, but she decided it did no one any good to condemn the baby for its mother's mistakes.

Linda was angry that her mother had had to rescue her, and that her boyfriend had turned out to be such an irresponsible jerk. Because she was more mature than most teenagers, or perhaps because she had grown up in a loving household, she nevertheless accepted the situation—relieved and testy at the same time. When she had the baby, her mother was with her through labor and delivery.

When I asked Linda how that felt, she replied, "Well, it wasn't like I'd imagined it to be. I always thought my husband would be going through childbirth with me. But I was glad Mom was there because she made me feel that everything would be okay in the end. Sometimes now, though, I get a little miffed at her—like maybe I think she's kept me from being independent. But I wasn't all that independent living in that apartment. Maybe by Mom's helping me now, I'll eventually *be* independent."

Then Linda smiled and added, "I hope *my* daughter behaves better as a teenager than I have."

Another girl had a different reaction. Diana had never had a close relationship with her mother. In fact, they had had a long-standing battle, with her mother accusing her of promiscuity and Diana accusing her mother of pushing her into it. When Diana found out that she was pregnant and her boyfriend refused to marry her, she assumed that her parents would take care of everything even if they weren't particularly happy about it. Though her mother suggested at first that she give the baby up for adoption, when Diana refused, she accepted her daughter's decision. However, she made it clear that she was done raising kids and wasn't about to incorporate Diana's baby into the family as if it were her own. She told Diana that it was in her best interest to live with a relative to have the baby so that neighbors wouldn't talk, but Diana felt that her mother was rejecting her. Diana's parents provided well for Diana materially, but when it came to emotional support, that had to come from Diana's aunt, with whom she lived until the baby was born.

Diana had mixed feelings about her family's support. She couldn't fault them for not helping her (they had bought all her maternity clothes and the baby's layette and paid for her prenatal care and delivery), but she still felt they had cast her aside. She sensed that she had let them down too, that she had done something wrong and set a bad example for her younger sister. She kept playing back her mother's words, "You're not going to ruin *my* life too, Diana."

Some of you who have had no help at all, or parents with little financial resources to help you, might feel that Diana was still lucky, that at least she was not bereft of financial assistance.

Here's another case where the teenager (a guy this time) lost the support of his mother because she couldn't condone what he was doing. Corey had never had a girlfriend until he met Trisha. After they had been dating a while and were sexually involved, Trisha's mother found out and demanded that they marry. By then, Trisha was pregnant, though there was a question as to who was the father. Corey dropped out of school intending to support his pregnant girlfriend. Margaret, his mother—a single parent of five—told me, "I didn't approve of this marriage, and I wasn't going to participate in his mistake."

Corey married Trisha, but from day one there were problems. Ironically, Corey was the one who was battered around, and he alternately went home to his mother to recoup from the abuse and returned to his wife to endure another round. Finally, his mother refused to let him come back unless he agreed to divorce Trisha. Margaret said she wanted Corey to wake up and see what was happening to his life. She thought that if she withdrew her support until he extricated himself from this mess, he would be more likely to come to his senses. She sadly told me, "I guess he thinks I deserted him, but I had to do what I thought was right."

Corey told me that he indeed felt deserted, not only by his mother but by his siblings, who didn't come to his aid either. Corey never actually tested his mother's resolve; he never appeared with suitcase in hand on her doorstep. Eventually he did tire of his situation, but the last I heard he was involved with yet another pregnant girlfriend.

On a brighter note, Aimee married her boyfriend when she was a couple of months pregnant. Not only did her mother and father rally around the couple, but so did Bradley's parents. Aimee and Bradley moved in with his parents to save money, and Bradley continued to attend high school and to work to help with expenses. Both sets of parents encouraged the couple to finish high school, and by helping to pay some bills and watching the baby after it was born, they made it possible for the teenagers to do just that. At this writing, a colleague tells me these teenagers have both graduated, they have a lovely baby girl, and they're buying a house. Aimee and Bradley beat the odds in establishing a solid marriage, conceived in a hurry though it was. They would probably tell you that it wouldn't have been possible without their parents' support and encouragement.

For those of you who have still not told your parents because: (1) you think the pregnancy might disappear on its own and then your parents would never have to know; or (2) they're going to be so angry that you don't want to deal with it, let me leave you with one last true but tragic story.

A few years ago in Portland, Maine, a young woman delivered her baby at home and then left him in a dumpster in the alley outside. Fortunately some kids passing by found the baby and called police, who rushed the baby to the hospital, where it survived. Why had this young girl done such an unspeakable thing?

She claimed she feared her parents would be mad at her for getting pregnant when she wasn't married. She never let on to anyone that she was pregnant, and because she was fat she never attracted undue notice.

Her parents were just as shocked as the community when they heard her explanation. This girl had jumped to the conclusion that because she had done something wrong, she would have to conceal the pregnancy and the baby that she delivered. It hadn't occurred to her to look elsewhere for assistance.

I know this case is extreme, but people who are scared sometimes do extreme things. If you feel you don't have your family behind you, it is *not* the end of the world. You are not a criminal for having gotten pregnant. You may have made a mistake, but I can't think of anyone I know who hasn't made at least one mistake in her life. If you have no family support, find the nearest family planning clinic and ask them to help you with services and resource people.

And for those of you who do have support, treasure it. Your parents are some of the best people in the world to have on your side.

CHAPTER 8

Physical and Emotional Changes

When I was first pregnant—and I was hardly a teenager at the time—I must have bought every book available that described the symptoms of pregnancy. I memorized whole passages, I read them so often. I was looking for some authority in those books to assure me that I was normal, that how I was feeling wasn't so very different from how every other pregnant woman felt.

I wasn't just comparing major symptoms either; I wasn't just worrying about normal little things. I had a lot of vivid dreams, and though my husband was preoccupied with how he was going to measure up as a father, I was preoccupied with how I would hold up during labor—*or even survive it.* Did anyone else in the whole world feel as I did?

Well, fortunately, the books concluded that someone did. All the books didn't mention each and every symptom and fear I had, but among twenty-five books I could usually find *someone* who had been in my shoes. It was reassuring to know that having a baby wasn't so new that someone else hadn't already experienced it all. I still remember the day my husband came home from work and found me curled up on the bathroom floor. He thought something was drastically wrong and ran over to disengage my hands from the toilet bowl.

"I can't do it," I told him between sobs. "I just can't do it."

"Can't do what?" he screamed.

"Go through labor," I said, crying harder.

"What do you mean?" he said. "You've got six more months to go!"

"Don't you see?" I cried, exasperated at his stupidity. "I have to get this settled now. I have to know that I'll be able to do it, that I can stand the pain and all."

"Everyone stands it," my sympathetic husband said. "You'll do just fine. I'll be there."

"I just wish *you* could go through it for me," I said.

That may sound funny to you. There I was, newly pregnant and already scared to death about labor. I thought I was the only person in the world who wondered if she could die.

The other day a colleague's fourteen-year-old client announced that she was pregnant. Later the girl asked her therapist, "Does anyone die in chidbirth anymore?"

Obviously other people *do* wonder about dying, and if it has ever flitted through your mind, don't worry. It doesn't mean that you're having a bad premonition or you've jinxed your delivery. It simply means that you're having a normal, frightened reaction. After all, you don't know your threshold of pain, and you don't know what your labor will be like. As I've mentioned elsewhere, it's normal to be scared of things you don't know.

You can do things about your fears; you don't have to live with them day in and day out. For one thing, you should begin prenatal care as soon as you suspect you might be pregnant. Having a doctor monitor your pregnancy, giving up drugs and alcohol that can cause birth defects—these steps will ease your mind about your baby's well-being. As for your own well-being, I suggest becoming an expert on yourself: your strengths, your weaknesses, and your concerns. You can help your doctor by cluing him in to your symptoms and fears. Share your concerns with him or her and the nurses who treat you. Make a list of questions to ask them about *anything* that bothers you. If you don't ask, doctors (who are usually overburdened as it is) will assume that you don't have any questions. Rare is the doctor who will take the time to pry questions out of a reluctant patient.

Sometimes you may not know exactly what is bothering you, only that something *is*. It's still important to tell the doctor that; most likely he or she has had similar young women patients and can help interpret what is upsetting you. Between visits, read as much on pregnancy as you can. I don't think a person can know too much. Usually the more you read, the more questions you'll have. But, believe me, it's better to ask the questions now, when everyone is relaxed and unhurried, than when you're writhing on the delivery table, saying, "Just a minute, I have a question. Just how much is all this going to hurt anyway?"

Before I became pregnant, I had worked with doctors all my adult life. They were psychiatrists, not obstetricians, but I still knew that doctors were no less human than the rest of the staff. As a social worker, I had argued many times with these psychiatrists over the care of our mutual patients. I had even fended off the advances of a few of them when I had been single. When you become pregnant, though, suddenly everything changes. It's as if you abdicate all rights to your body, and you just naturally assume that the doctor knows best.

On one level, I knew that doctors were mortals and subject to bad days. On a very different level, I expected them to be omniscient about my pregnancy. I was embarrassed to ask questions for two reasons: I might say something stupid and they'd laugh at me, and I might waste their valuable time with small concerns.

Let me assure you, if a doctor trivializes your concerns, you need to switch doctors. The doctor is there to serve *you*. *You* keep him in business. You actually make his or her job easier by asking questions, pointing out your concerns, and demonstrating that you're not the passive patient who will blindly accept everything he or she says.

When I realized that the doctor wasn't taking me seriously, I took a good look at my own behavior. I discovered that when *I* took myself more seriously, questioning the things I did not understand, the doctor took me more seriously. Don't expect your doctor to be a god. He is a professional with whom you are working. The fact that you're younger than many pregnant women doesn't mean you have no right to be part of the treatment.

Lamaze classes are another source of information and support. You attend these classes in your last trimester, when the information about childbirth will be of more interest and relevance. Taking these classes doesn't mean you have to have an unmedicated labor. Of the ten couples in my Lamaze class, only two women had our babies naturally. The others were just as happy with their anesthesia and caesarean sections.

The thing I liked best about the classes was the sense of having others go through this experience with me. Your friends can stand only so much talk about the baby or the pregnancy blues, but at these groups we were gathered together for that express purpose. Even now I look back on those other couples as allies.

You may have heard pregnancy referred to as a roller coaster ride. My only objection to that comparison is that most people think roller coasters are *fun* to ride, and for some women pregnancy isn't fun at all. Be that as it may, let me give you a brief overview of some of the physical and emotional symptoms of pregnancy. Bear in mind that you may not have all these symptoms, particularly the emotional ones, because your attitude toward the pregnancy may be different. Perhaps I won't touch on the way you're feeling. Don't interpret that to mean that no one else feels that particular way. It simply means that no one mentioned it to me when I was cataloging the ways many people felt. Before you start worrying about your particular symptom, mention it to your doctor. Chances are, you're still as normal as they come.

Some women report feeling tired a lot when they're pregnant. Things people say make them want to cry, and their friends tell you they're more irritable than they ever were. They've lost their sense of humor; they've lost their "perspective." Usually these personality changes result from the higher level of hormones coursing through their body. Less commonly, the moods are a result of their feelings about the pregnancy. If that is the case with you, it's helpful to talk over what is bothering you with a trusted friend—perhaps someone who has been in your situation.

Some women "glow" during pregnancy. Their skin clears up (those hormones again), and they just plain feel wonderful. I can't describe that experience in good detail because I never was one of those people. I was one for whom the whole experience precipitated depression. The only good thing about it was that I never had postpartum depression, perhaps because I was not attached to the pregnancy itself, but rather—the baby.

How you tolerate your body's changing right before your eyes (and your boyfriend's or husband's) probably has a lot to do with how secure you are about your appearance before you become pregnant. I had always been afraid of getting overweight. (I was never so humiliated as when, in fifth grade, a salesclerk suggested to my mother that she look for dresses for me in the "chubby" department.) Periodically, my weight had gotten the better of me, but in my second marriage I had been very attentive to my weight. You can imagine my horror at seeing my belly take off on its own when I was pregnant. At first my waist got thicker, so that when I sat behind a desk at work I had to unsnap my pants so I could breathe. I was too small for maternity clothes, but my regular clothes were straining at the seams. I considered making a sign reading. "I'm not fat. I'm pregnant."

Nobody told me I was going to feel foolish at first wearing pants with this huge elastic panel in front. The day I tried them on at home, my husband watched in fascination—no doubt wondering how long it would be before I filled out the roomy front panel. I thought I saw him smiling. That was the first time I considered getting dressed in the closet . . .

I remember the first time I stood sideways at the mirror. *With no clothes on.* I looked grotesque. I tried to suck in my stomach. Nothing happened. I pushed on it, and it was hard. Then I caught my husband staring at me from the hallway, and he had that awful smirk on his face. I tried to hide.

"Oh, come on," he said. "You look beautiful. I think your belly's beautiful."

"You're just saying that," I said, but I did peer back in the mirror to see if my sloping belly might not look attractive.

It didn't.

"Well, it's not fat," I assured him. "And it'll go away."

"I know," he said.

If anyone tells you that you look beautiful when your belly is growing beyond your control and you waddle when you walk, cherish that friendship. Your ego needs to hear stuff like that, even if you don't believe a word of it.

I think the phrase that best typifies pregnancy is "loss of control." So many little things start to plague you once you're pregnant, things over which you have little or no control. To maintain your sanity, you'll probably have to decide early on that some of these things are just minor inconveniences. You're going to be running to the bathroom a lot in the beginning and toward the end of pregnancy. That is because your uterus is pressing against your bladder; whatever your bladder capacity has been in the past, it will be much less now. You may notice your breasts tingling at first, much as they do before your period starts. But this feeling will not go away after a few days. Your breasts will become fuller, and later your nipples will darken. Along with the darkening nipples, you might see a dark brown line down the center of your chest and abdomen, as if someone had drawn a mark to cut you in two. Books say that the line will fade but not go away afterward. (I just looked at mine; it has disappeared, though it was present during each of my pregnancies.)

Many people either feel nausea or actually vomit during the first trimester of pregnancy. Doctors attribute the queasy stomach to the increased hormones, which certainly won't make you feel any less queasy. Munching dry crackers or toast helps. Probably anything mild in the stomach will help. I've read that apricot juice would help too, but its texture (thick and syrupy) actually made me worse. If you can't find anything to munch on that you can keep down (even a popsicle), tell your doctor. You shouldn't go too long without nourishing your body. After all, your sustenance is the baby's too.

That leads me to another topic that I might as well delve into now. We've only recently become aware of just how dangerous chemicals like drugs and alcohol can be to a developing fetus. You may not realize how crucial those first three months of pregnancy are to your baby's development. The fetus develops its brain, organs, and limbs in the first trimester. If you take something that alters the fetus's immediate environment, those parts of its body will not develop properly. *What doesn't develop on schedule won't develop later.* Your baby won't get a second chance. Alcohol crosses the placenta; whatever you drink, the baby drinks in. Your adult liver can filter out the alcohol from the bloodstream, but the baby's immature liver cannot. He literally goes swimming in alcohol. Alcohol will affect your baby's brain development, and that is something that can never be undone.

Babies born to mothers who were heavy drinkers during pregnancy may have what is called fetal alcohol syndrome. They are smaller than normal babies, have slower reflexes and possibly retarded motor development, impaired judgment, and other serious defects. *There is no cure for this. Only prevention.* Even small amounts of alcohol regularly consumed by the pregnant mother may lead to babies born with fetal alcohol effect, who suffer similar problems though to a lesser degree.

Don't take chances with your baby's life. Don't drink.

Smoking reduces the amount of oxygen reaching the fetus. Every time you inhale, the baby suffers. Since the fetus suddenly receives less oxygen, he may suffer respiratory problems at birth and be at greater risk to die from SIDS. Recently, researchers have been able to document the dangers of *secondhand smoke*. If you don't smoke but are in rooms or cars with people who do, your baby is still at risk. Breathing in a roomful of smoky air compromises your baby's development just as much as if you were the one smoking.

Babies born cocaine-addicted are even more pitiful: premature babies, no bigger than your hand, suffering very real and painful symptoms of cocaine withdrawal. If you can't stop using on your own, admit yourself to a drug treatment center and get help. You are already going to have a hard time raising an infant at your age. Don't make things harder by having to raise a *handicapped* baby.

A friend of mine suggested that I tell you all the physical complications of pregnancy, so that you'll take your doctor's advice more seriously. She is a woman whose teeth were destroyed from lack of vitamins and proper nutrition in her frequent pregnancies. She now has heart trouble brought on by lack of care in her teenage pregnancies.

"If I had been told these things could happen," Margaret said, "I'd have been more attentive."

"What would you have done if your doctor had told you these things?" I asked, "Would you have believed him?"

"Well, no, I probably wouldn't have listened to him," she admitted. "But if literature had been available in the waiting room, I'd have read that."

From my observation, it is hard for us as professionals

to impart any "wisdom" to teenagers, mostly because they aren't listening. I know that because I was once a teenager and I didn't listen to adults either. But you'll have to trust me on this one: Doctors and nurses *do know* what they're talking about when they advise you about health in pregnancy. It won't hurt you to follow a balanced diet and give up drugs, but I can assure you, it *will* hurt if you don't.

As you progress through pregnancy, you may find yourself increasingly fatigued. It's another "one of those things" that you'll just have to accept. Some people feel a resurgence of "well-being" during the middle months, and of course the proverbial burst of energy just before going into labor. If you're one of those who gets tired a lot, take frequent naps and rest as much as possible. There won't be much time for that afterward.

As I mentioned, depending on your stature, your waist will start to thicken somewhere between three and four and a half months, and eventually your belly will start to enlarge. Try as you may to hold it in, it won't budge an inch, and it will feel hard. Toward the end of your fourth month, maybe even into your fifth month, you may feel some funny flutterings in your abdomen. At first they'll be only occasional, but as the baby grows larger and your awareness increases, you'll notice these movements regularly during the day and especially at night. Babies seem to be nocturnal creatures. Maybe it's just that when you're lying still you notice the jostling more. In any event, don't count on getting a lot of sleep at night after you're in the last stages of pregnancy.

Not everyone develops stretch marks. I've had four pregnancies, spaced fairly close together, and have never had a stretch mark. (Scientists say it has something to do with skin elasticity and genetics.) I don't know what difference it really makes. It's not as if I'm about to parade my body around, showing off my lack of stretch marks. They don't show through clothes, for one thing, and for another, there comes the point in every *old woman's life* when it's time to trade in the bikini. Stretch marks may look ugly during the pregnancy—sometimes purply-red lines running in all directions from the navel. After the baby is born, they'll fade until they're pearly white and relatively inconspicuous.

Here are some more problems that face you in pregnancy. Colostrum will leak from your breasts (after the nineteenth week) in preparation for nursing your baby. You may experience hemorrhoids, varicose veins, frequent nosebleeds, headaches, nasal congestion and swelling of your feet and ankles. I had some really horrible headaches that were for the most part caused by head congestion. Everything seems to get stopped up when you're pregnant. Your head hurts, your body swells all over, and you can't have a bowel movement without swallowing a gallon of castor oil first. (I'm only kidding about the castor oil. Watch out for taking laxatives, especially before labor, no matter how many women tell you it will bring on contractions.) Again, you'll just have to take my word for it. This too shall pass.

You can have some weird dreams when you're pregnant. Women have told me that they dreamed about themselves as mothers or about giving birth to a grotesque animal instead of a baby. Don't worry; it's just your body's way of exploring your fears during pregnancy. My son was stillborn in my second pregnancy, and when I was pregnant with the following child, I worried that it too would die. One night I dreamed that I had had the baby and it ran away from me. Only the baby was now a toddler who was climbing some stairs to get away. Up, up, up he went. I struggled to follow, but he kept getting farther ahead. Finally I got to the top of the stairs and saw a huge swimming pool toward which my baby was running. Just as certainly as I knew the baby would fall in, I knew I could not reach him in time to save him. Helplessly, I called to him to stop. Just then he toppled in, but right beside the pool appeared a woman who reached in and pulled my baby out. I awoke with a tremendous feeling of relief. I knew that this time, even if my unborn baby experienced difficulties, someone would save him in time. Which is what happened.

At the end of your pregnancy, just when you're certain you can't endure another indignity, you may have these things to contend with: a need to urinate even more frequently and sometimes failing to make it to the bathroom in time. Your navel will pop out, and you'll swear your belly will explode if it expands one more inch. People may accuse you of having swallowed a basketball. You may be embarrassed if you're wearing a tight-fitting (everything is tight-fitting at this point) sweater and these funny little movements jump across the width of your belly as if a mole were burrowing under your clothes. If you sit down on a couch, you may have to stay there a while until someone comes along to pull you up on your feet. You might get stuck in the bathtub too. I'm not kidding! (I lived in mortal fear that that would happen to me and I'd be forced to yell to my elderly male neighbor to rescue me.) When you look down at your toes, they won't be there anymore. In fact, your feet will have disappeared too. All you'll see is this immense, round belly overtaking your body.

When you're far along in your pregnancy, you may feel more dependent on others, such as your boyfriend, husband, or mother. It's a normal part of pregnancy.

Women naturally feel vulnerable with a life growing inside them. Some women become nervous when their husband leaves to go to work. You can project your fear for the baby's safety onto your boyfriend or husband, so that you worry about his getting hurt or killed and leaving you alone to contend with this pregnancy. It's a normal reaction; usually it passes after childbirth.

Pregnancy isn't all bad. Some women truly feel a glow. They feel special and at peace, and it shows in everything they do. These women don't even seem to waddle in the last month of pregnancy. Do hormones upset these women less, or is it their attitude? I don't know. These are the women, though, who caress their stomach and talk to the baby. They fantasize about the baby and themselves, and in general they enjoy all the attention. They even enjoy the baby's every squirm, interpreting the punches and jabs not as "punches and jabs" but as the miracle of creation.

Perhaps you're in the middle somewhere, marveling one day at this process of life and hating it the next. Nothing is black and white. Pregnancy is neither all fun and games nor a tedious undertaking. If you think I have dwelt too much on the "down" side, it's only because you don't need help coping with the "good" experiences. If you enjoy the whole process, good for you! If pregnancy depresses you, relax. It won't last forever, and you're not a "bad mother" for resenting the intrusion into your body. You don't necessarily hate the baby simply because you hate the experience of pregnancy.

But believe me, if you hang onto your sense of humor, you'll weather the whole thing with your sanity intact.

THE MALE PERSPECTIVE

Even though the physical experience is out of your realm, that very fact may make it all the more intolerable. You will watch your girlfriend, or wife, become moodier and perhaps more demanding. If you are not expecting this, you may take it personally. Reread the previous section if you aren't aware of what happens to a woman during pregnancy. Realize, too, that these changes are caused in part by "raging hormones" and in part by the woman's positive or negative attitude about her experience. It may also reflect her being too tired to exert much control over her increasingly fluctuating moods. (Pointing these facts out to her—even with good intent—usually makes matters worse. A woman already knows she is behaving unpredictably. It doesn't help to tell her it must be "one of those woman things.")

Some guys are actually "turned on" by the sight of a pregnant woman. Not all guys are repulsed by the temporary change in shape. Some told me they were afraid of hurting the woman or the baby if they continued to have sex. Unless the doctor gives a medical reason to abstain from sex (such as premature bleeding or pain), you should be able to enjoy sex all the way through the pregnancy. The woman's belly will begin to pose a problem after several months, but then you just have to explore other ways around it. You don't have to stop.

Some guys are confused about their role. "What should I be doing?"

I can't help you on that one, guys. It depends on the woman. What does *she* want of you? Ask her.

Other guys don't treat their girlfriend or wife differently for a while. That is in part, I've been told, because it's easier at first for a man to deny the pregnancy, which isn't as apparent to him as it is to the woman who can feel the changes inside her. About the time the man begins to notice the belly changing shape and hardening, he begins to realize, "She really is pregnant after all." Then he may start treating her like a fragile doll, just when she's enjoying the pregnancy and the freedom from those horrible first months of nausea.

As a couple, you can do several things to lessen the trauma of changing from a couple to parents. First of all, both of you must open up. Tell each other how you are feeling, what you're worried about, what you feel good about. Guys do not automatically know how it feels to be pregnant just because they've seen their sister or their mother go through it. You are different, and you must tell him what it's like for *you*. Likewise, you don't know what your husband or boyfriend thinks about it unless you ask him to share his feelings.

During my third pregnancy I kept a journal of my feelings. I noted every little nuance; I wrote down every single thought I had. After a few weeks I noticed that I was always talking about what the experience was like for *me*—having lost a child and now having conceived again. Over all those pages there was no note of what my husband was feeling about this pregnancy, although he had lost the same child and was again going through this with me. I remember wondering, "Is he not talking to me, or am I just not listening?"

For your own information and to support your wife or girlfriend, I'm all for accompanying her to the doctor appointments. I hate to say this, but I've observed it myself: Some doctors are more attentive when a support person is with the teenager. Perhaps it is because the doctor feels he or she is being monitored by a third party. Perhaps it is because he has considered the teenager's questions petty in the past but is more amenable to talking with a guy or an adult. Whatever the circumstances, take time out, guys, to go with her to the doctor. You'll learn a lot and be that much more at ease when you face the doctor in the delivery room.

Take Lamaze classes with your wife or girlfriend. As I've mentioned, these groups are a wonderful source of information and support. Sometimes the men seem to benefit most because other guys are in their very same circumstances. The classes can help prepare the guy for the surprises of labor, but only if he does not expect his wife or girlfriend to follow exactly any scenarios he has been told about.

I remember my husband's phoning our Lamaze instructor while I was in the throes of labor. I heard him holler into the phone, "She's not doing the breathing right; it's not going according to plan."

Well, of course it wasn't; childbirth never follows anyone's plan. The classes merely give you a format to ask questions about pregnancy and delivery. You learn special relaxation techniques to prepare you for labor and to help tune in to each other. Enjoy these classes and the people in them. They are merely to help.

One last thing. If you don't have the support of your boyfriend or the interest of your husband, find someone else to go through the experience of childbirth with you: your mother, a trusted friend, a sister. This is a time when you don't need to be alone; you need all the support you can get. Even if physically you do it all yourself, you can always use the positive energy of someone you love and trust.

PART · III

LOSSES IN PREGNANCY

CHAPTER ◇ 9

Lost Babies

This chapter will probably be the hardest one for you to read, because it deals with something going wrong in your pregnancy. I include the chapter, however, because of the 180,000 American teenagers who lose babies each year through miscarriage, stillbirth, or neonatal death.

Many people shake their heads at the staggering number of teenagers giving birth each year— over one million, according to recent figures. These same people don't seem concerned by the effects of the untold losses each year— 180,000 deaths, 400,000 abortions, and some 38,000 babies who will die before reaching their first birthday—their death in large part because of their mother's inadequate prenatal care.

My intent in writing this chapter is simply to recognize these losses; to let you look at your pain, if you have suffered one of these losses, and then to let it go. If it helps you to know that I have lost a child too, you may be relieved to know that I've survived the loss.

For those of you who are reading this chapter because you have lost a baby, my heart goes out to you. You will be forever different. For those of you who are reading it because a friend has lost a baby, let me assure you that the greatest favor you can do your friend is to let her grieve. And listen. And listen. And listen some more.

First, let me clarify some terms. A miscarriage is the expelling of the fetus before it is able to survive (from a day-old pregnancy ending in blood and tissue to a five-month pregnancy ending in a more recognizable fetus). A stillbirth occurs when an infant dies before birth, and a neonatal death occurs when an infant dies in the hours or days just following birth.

When a teenager loses a baby, most of society is relieved to be rid of the problem. Some assume that the teenager herself is too inexperienced in life to realize what she has lost, that since her circumstances would have been so negatively altered by the birth of the child, she is probably relieved to be rid of it. The only thing wrong with this line of thinking is that even if the girl were relieved, there would still be immeasurable guilt in being relieved.

A loss is a loss, whether it happens to a thirteen-year-old girl or a thirty-year-old woman. Neither age nor marital status insulates a person from pain. The older, more mature woman may merely be better at articulating that loss.

When I was in high school, a girl I had grown up with—one in my junior class—got pregnant, married, and left school. In that order. It happened not so infrequently, so it really wasn't such a big deal.

Months later we heard that the baby died at birth. For us, the shock lay in the unthinkable having happened. And then we thought, collectively at least, "Too bad Susan married so fast. Now she has no reason to stay married."

It never occurred to most of us that someone—a baby—had just *died*. And that the parents—even if they were only seventeen years old—were just as shaken as older ones would have been.

I thought of this girl years later when my own son died at birth. I realized with belated awareness how much pain Susan must have felt. No matter that she was young enough to have several more kids in the future. That one—that particular one—was gone. The loss, the emptiness, and the rage must all have been there.

The reactions to a loss are as varied as the reasons for a person's getting pregnant in the first place. To some extent your reaction reflects how important the pregnancy was to you or how real it had become. Let me tell you about my own case.

My son was stillborn when I was 38 weeks pregnant. (At term is considered anywhere from 38 to 42 weeks.) I had had a normal pregnancy; I was healthy, had never smoked, and didn't use drugs or alcohol. In fact, I hadn't heard of anyone in my circumstances losing a baby like this. The baby was delivered at 4 a.m., and in a blessed state of oversedation I slept away the rest of the morning. When I awoke, I couldn't remember at first where I was or why I was there. And then it hit me as though I had been punched in the stomach. *My son was dead.* I saw all these tubes sticking out of me and liquids running into me, and I tried to focus on the physical pain to block out the ice-cold panic creeping through me. I thought of the words in the song: "Nobody knows it's the end of the world..." because the sun was shining and birds were flitting by my window as if nothing extraordinary had happened that day.

After a while the numbness started to wear off, and I went a little crazy from the anger festering inside. There was so much free-floating anger that I hardly knew where to begin. I hated all the people who told me not to worry, that I could always conceive again. And all the people who said, "It must have been God's will," as if anyone would have willed for a baby to die inside its mother. I even hated all the other pregnant women in the world who were blissfully going about their pregnancies.

I didn't move through the stages of grief in any consistent manner. Some days I was so angry I could barely see straight—thinking things like, "Why *me*? What have I done to deserve this?" Other days all I wanted to do was curl up in bed and sleep for a hundred years, not waking up until the pain was gone. (At those times, drugs would have been an all-too-easy way to cover up the pain.)

"If I could just not remember," I told myself, but there were reminders everywhere: other infants, all the baby things I had accumulated, and the date staring at me from the wall calendar. Sometimes I thought the whole thing was a bad dream, and that if I could only wake up I'd see that my son hadn't died after all.

I felt guilty too. Doctors never found out why my son had died. "It was just one of those things," they said.

So there I was, with all this anger and no one to blame. Part of me believed it must have been my fault. After all, I was the mother; I should have known something was wrong. I flogged myself with my ambivalence during the pregnancy. Had I done something wrong? The night before our son died my husband and I had argued about my overspending on baby clothes. Had our angry feelings somehow hurt the baby? Why hadn't I known? Surely *that* was my fault.

Coupled with the feelings of anger, shock, and guilt was the (at times) intense desire to conceive again. Not just to see if I could have another child, but also to rectify my failure. Maybe this time I would do it right...

The loss of my son was the most wrenching, horrible

thing that has ever happened to me, and yet society treated me with respect and caring. That was because I was happily married and stable enough to provide for a child. That support caused me to wonder about the unwed pregnant teenager, for whom an unplanned pregnancy was such a negative thing. How would an unwed teenager get any empathy—any recognition of her pain—so that she wouldn't feel compelled to rush right out and become pregnant again.

More often than not, society does not really believe that you—the teenager—grieve a miscarriage or stillborn child, nor does it typically believe that anything significant has been lost. After all, it is not as if you had come to know the child.

What society doesn't realize is that you may already have bonded with the unborn child, with the fantasy of being its mother, and that now not only is the child gone but also the promise of motherhood and the innocence of a safe pregnancy thereafter.

Of course, there are different levels of awareness, and different ways that people respond to a loss. The twelve-year-old who doesn't realize she's pregnant until an early miscarriage brings the fact to light will probably feel less grief than the seventeen-year-old girl who has wanted the pregnancy and loses the child after six or seven months.

For those of you who claim to feel nothing at all over your loss, I suggest you dig a little deeper into your feelings past all that denial. Numbness and denial serve a purpose—essentially to spare you the pain of awareness. Unfortunately, ignoring the pain, insulating yourself against it, will not make the pain go away, any more than drugs and alcohol will alter the problems they're supposed to be easing. You are never entirely free from the pain of loss, *even if you choose not to look at it.*

I once worked with a woman in one of my groups who told the group one evening that that day was her dead son's birthday. This woman was in her late sixties, but not a year had gone by that she hadn't remembered her dead son's birthday. He had been stillborn forty-eight years before.

Another woman, hospitalized and dying of cancer late in life, told a nurse that she wasn't afraid to die because "Now I will see my babies again." This woman had ten living children, numerous grandchildren, and even a few great-grandchildren. Still she remembered the dates of her two miscarriages (at least sixty years earlier) and her son's stillbirth. "I never stopped grieving for those babies," she said, although her life appeared rich with love and fulfillment.

For those of you who have suffered a miscarriage, still-birth, or neonatal death, I am not condemning you to months of agony. What I am saying is that losing some-one *hurts*, and that it is okay to feel pain and anger, even if having that child might have seemed the most tragic mistake of your young life. Grieving will *not* kill you, and it will not torment you forever if you deal with it.

Speaking of guilt, what about the stillbirths and neonatal deaths caused by the mothers' lack of prenatal care or her abuse of drugs and alcohol?

If that has been your case, you will have to confront your own part (through ignorance or negligence) in the death, and *then* your sadness and pain at the loss. It can be hoped that you will learn from this tragedy and ultimately forgive yourself and get on with life.

A special kind of loss comes with abortion, because you have purposely chosen to terminate the pregnancy. Be-cause of your part, you have to separate out the guilt before you can reach the pain. Many people opting for abortion deny that it was a big deal. Some admit that they regret it;

but they are also quick to say that they had no other choice. It had to be done, as if its urgency negates the pain of loss. My point isn't that you should not have had the abortion (that is a decision only *you* can make); it is that no matter what else, the unborn child was part of you, and now it is gone.

Over the years I have seen scores of women who have had abortions. They were from every social class, though abortion tends to be more a middle- and upper-class solution to an unplanned pregnancy. The one thing that all these women (including teenagers) had in common was their regret. That is not to say that all of them would have gone on to bear the child; most would still have had the abortion. However, their choice haunted them over the years, and they often wondered what the child might have looked like. Even though they had precipitated the loss, they still grieved it.

One of the problems with abortions is that often they have been done in secrecy. You can't share your feelings with others when you haven't revealed the event that caused them. Just when you need emotional support the most, you have closed yourself off from it by pretending the event never happened.

Faith was an attractive teenager when she became pregnant. Having been brought up in the Bible Belt of Oklahoma, she felt guilty and trapped by her dilemma. Having a baby as an unwed mother was almost as frowned upon as aborting it; the first was flouting the morals of the community; the second was violating the sanctity of life. Faith nonetheless chose to have an abortion in secrecy. She moved away from home to attend college but evidently never found the peace of mind she was seeking. She grew obese and used that as a way to avoid intimacy and the possibility of becoming pregnant again. I last saw Faith several years ago. She had become very religious, almost as if she were doing penance for an act for which she never forgave herself. She rarely discussed what she had done, and when she did, it was to focus on her guilt, not her grief.

A therapist once asked me (when I was wallowing in anger and self-pity), "if you took away the guilt and anger, what would you have left?"

For a moment I was silent. What was the guilt and anger keeping me from feeling? And then it hit me, as if a truck had plowed right into me. *Emptiness, loss.* It was much easier to be mad than to ache.

Anger is pervasive. You may be mad at yourself for not producing a healthy child, at your boyfriend/husband for making you pregnant, and at that same guy for not sharing your loss. (Sometimes I felt that our stillborn son was my loss alone; after all, my husband had not shared the physical trauma of delivering a dead baby. He hadn't felt the life inside him those thirty-eight weeks.)

Sometimes you may feel angry becuase no one seems to care that you hurt or that the baby died in the first place. And invariably you feel angry at everyone who has gone on to deliver healthy babies. I never saw so many pregnant women or infants in my life as I did after we lost our son. I resented them all—even the infants, because they were not my son.

Several colleagues at my office were also pregnant when my son died. I felt I was being additionally singled out for punishment, having to face them each day. Some of the women I tried to avoid—especially their babies, who only reminded me of my loss.

It was harder to avoid my best friend, who once accused me of spoiling the joy of *her* pregnancy. Ultimately I had to confront and accept my loss so that I could keep her friendship. But for a long time I was afraid to hold her baby, afraid of my fears and desire, ashamed that I was being disloyal to my dead son. It took a lot of guts, not only for me to hang onto this friendship, but for Janet not to recoil from my experience.

You may have girlfriends who have carried pregnancies to term, and only you can decide if you should struggle to maintain the friendship or put it temporarily on hold.

Now believe it or not, even with all my ignoble feelings, I was not crazy. And *you* are not crazy just because you have them too. You may feel like snatching someone else's baby. As long as the vengeful fantasy remains a fantasy, you don't have to condemn yourself for it. *You just don't act on it.*

Anger is one thing; grief and longing are far harder to endure. After my son died, I experienced waves of longing to hold him. Not to hold someone else's baby. To hold *him*. There I was, over thirty years old with two college degrees, but I still found myself lapsing into fanciful thinking to get him back. I remember once writing in my journal, "If there's a God as my mother believes, I'd like to strike a deal with Him: whatever it takes to go back in time and retrieve my son."

I couldn't stand feeling so empty and sad. I wanted to hurry up and get pregnant again—perhaps to replace the lost child, but also to undo my failure.

There's a different kind of grieving with adoption. With this arrangement, your child is never entirely gone, although he or she is gone from your present life. There is enormous guilt: Did I do the right thing? Will he or she understand when grown-up? Will the adoptive parents treat him or her okay?

There are feelings of longing (for what cannot be), regret

(guilt), resignation ("There was nothing else I could do") and relief ("Now I can get on with my life"). Of course, as I mentioned earlier, guilt is usually mixed in with relief, as if you shouldn't feel good about something so bad.

Teenage fathers can feel any of the above feelings to the degree that they were attached to their girlfriend and their fantasy child. In general, there is a three-month lag with men in the recognition of a pregnancy. Men often don't conceptualize the pregnancy (although they rationally accept it) until it is a visible thing (usually in the second trimester.) Most miscarriages take place in the first trimester, so that the man won't have the awareness or bonding that the woman has at that point.

I think with teenagers especially there is an element of shock and disbelief. The surprise of getting pregnant in the first place ("I didn't think it could happen to us") gives way to the shock of death in this day and age ("She did everything right; how could this have happened?").

After my son's death I initially thought my husband hated me. I thought he blamed me for our son's death, that he probably couldn't stand being around me. I even had fantasies that he wanted to leave me, until I gradually realized that it was I who was doing all the hating and blaming. All the horrible thoughts I attributed to him were really things I was feeling about myself. Once I accepted that, I could see through to my husband's grief and include him in my struggle to get beyond the loss.

In most cases, society is less responsive to men who have lost children, seeming to view the early loss as women's. And as I've mentioned, to an unwed teenager, society seems to see it as almost no loss at all.

How do you prevent losses such as miscarriages and stillbirths?

Well, unfortuantely, you can't prevent them all. Some

pregnancies are meant to be lost because something is wrong with the developing fetus. Some things are simply unexplainable, beyond your control. Aside from that, what you can do to ensure a healthy pregnancy is to receive prompt prenatal care and to avoid all substances dangerous to the fetus.

How do you cope with a loss? For one thing, you must recognize and acknowledge your feelings, whatever they may be (which means *feeling* them, not simply *naming* the feelings; there's a difference). You let yourself feel whatever it is you're feeling, not what society tells you to feel, and not even necessarily what I have mentioned here. Sometimes it's useful to keep a journal of your feelings. Putting your feelings on paper has a purging effect.

The next step is to talk about it with a concerned adult or a peer. Sharing your feelings is a way of sorting them out, getting some perspective, and halving the pain.

If your baby dies in the hospital, there are ways to lessen the trauma of your hospital stay. The nursing staff should already have separated you from the other new mothers so that you won't have to cope with the sights and sounds of motherhood. If they haven't done so and it bothers you to be near the newborns, ask the staff to move you. You have that right. Seek out the nurses, who may be hesitant to approach you about your loss. They are there to talk with you, not just monitor your blood pressure—and they are usually all too familiar with the experience of infant death.

Following my son's stillbirth I was in the hospital an additional twenty-four hours, because I had had a saddle block during delivery and needed to lie flat for a time until the effect of the anesthesia wore off. Fortunately I had a private room in the gynecological wing (where everyone was having tubal ligations or hysterectomies), so I didn't have to deal with other new mothers cooing over infants.

Everything went smoothly until I was leaving. Then a nurse (eager to get me out of there, bless her heart) caught an elevator that was already heading down. She rolled me onto that elevator before we noticed the other occupants: a nurse behind the wheelchair of a young mother and newborn. I stared straight ahead at the control buttons and willed myself to keep breathing during the eight floors it took to get down. We exited together—that young woman with her daughter, and I with my son's stillbirth certificate. It was just one of those things. . .

Sometimes it is important to view and have a service for the dead child, if he or she were stillborn or died shortly after birth. Depending on your maturity, sometimes having a fetus (of a miscarriage) buried puts some closure on the event. In any case, I encourage the professional to discuss the options with you, to support you but not to take over for you if he or she can avoid it. You were capable of becoming pregnant and being a mother; you are capable of handling the death.

If you are choking on anger, and most people are at some point, the best thing to do is to mobilize all that emotion. Find an appropriate channel by:

1. Joining a peer support group to help others facing what you've been through. (You can find these through your YWCA, school, or church.)
2. Taking up a sport or hobby (preferably one that will sap your energy.)
3. Setting some *positive* short-term goal and working toward it. (And getting pregnant again isn't one.)

You will feel sad. There's no way around that. Some experts say that grieving should last six months. I don't think there is a specific time period, because people's ability to handle tragedy differs greatly. But certainly if you are still finding it impossible to get out of bed in the morning several months after the loss, or if you're using drugs or alcohol to dull the pain, you need professional help. If you're wondering why bother going on with life at all, you need professional help *at once*. Professionals are trained to help people deal with the painful stages of recovery, and they can help *you*—no matter what your ability to pay for the therapy. In the next chapter I describe some of the various kinds of counselors.

You *can cope* if you follow a few bits of advice. If you're sad, the worst thing you can do is bottle it up. Instead, talk to concerned adults and peers. If you're seriously depressed or suicidal, call a counseling agency, the hospital, your guidance counselor, your minister, or all of the above. Don't be in a hurry to get pregnant again. You have plenty of time to conceive again when circumstances are better and you're not trying to replace the lost child.

Last of all, I can't guarantee that the pain will go away, but I know *you can live through it*. I have . . .

People to Help You

W hen I was going through a divorce, I wanted to find a therapist with whom I could work through my anger and rage. But whom should I see? Not only that; what kind of person should I see? A psychiatrist, a psychologist, a social worker, a minister? How about the woman downtown who had a sign in her window: Specialist in Problems of the Newly Single. What did that mean anyway? What guarantee did I have that these people wouldn't just take my money and run? Or make me feel *worse*?

Finding the right therapist can seem as confusing as the problems propelling you into counseling in the first place. Briefly, let me explain, then, how the four main types of therapists differ. Then I'll offer some thoughts on how you can go about selecting one with whom you're comfortable, and what you can reasonably expect therapy to do for you.

A psychiatrist is not only a therapist, but a medical doctor as well. That means that only this person can prescribe medicine for you if your problem (anxiety, depression, whatever) requires the use of medication. A licensed psychiatrist has gone through medical school and earned a state medical license (usually requiring passage of an examination and a year of internship.) Many psychiatrists have completed three additional years of residency in psychiatry, for a total of four years of graduate work after medical school.

Now what does that mean to you? Well, if your problem requires medical attention for the treatment of severe depression (for example) or significantly disturbed thinking, you might be referred to a psychiatrist. It is costly, upward of $100 an hour. Reputable psychiatrists, however, are affiliated with counseling agencies as well as having private practice, so you can see them at reduced fees. But you do not need a psychiatrist simply because you believe that specialist is the cream of the crop of the medical profession. Many other professionals are equally qualified to help you, and if in the end they feel you need the expertise of a psychiatrist, they can work in conjunction with one in your treatment.

A psychologist is also a doctor, but cannot prescribe medicine. Usually a psychologist has either a PhD (doctorate in psychology) or an EdD (doctorate in education and counseling) and has had four to five years of college at the graduate level. To be licensed, he or she must have had an additional two years of supervised counseling experience. Just as with psychiatrists, he or she can belong to organizations that will monitor his or her behavior. Those organizations are to your benefit, of course. A psychologist can administer tests to assess a person's strengths and weaknesses and has the knowledge to interpret and use the results. Naturally, a psychologist is expensive unless seen at a clinic, which can reduce the fees based on your ability to pay. Don't worry; that in no way means that the quality of care will be compromised.

I had always thought that social workers were people

who doled out welfare checks and then followed up to make sure you spent the money wisely. Well, there are other kinds of social workers, trained as counselors, who specialize in family therapy or substance-abuse counseling. To be licensed, a social worker must have a master's in social work (MSW) and have completed two years of postgraduate study and two years of supervised practice. Some social workers hold a doctorate as well. In most states he or she must pass a written exam. Social workers, like their colleagues in psychiatry and psychology, can be seen in private practice or in clinics for reduced fees. Their individual differences reflect more their specialization in practice than their inherent ability.

Lastly, there are psychiatric nurses, often called clinical nurse specialists. They have a degree in nursing (preferably a BS) plus a master's in psychiatric and mental health nursing or in counseling. They must pass a state licensing examination to practice as a professional registered nurse, and after two years of postgraduate experience they may take the exam for certification as a clinical specialist. You can find clinical nurse specialists in a clinic setting or working in private practice with a doctor. Their fees vary.

That is a quick rundown on the people who are qualified to help you by virture of their mental health training. Of course, there are ministers trained in counseling, and substance-abuse counselors who may not have postgraduate training. There are also people who call themselves counselors though they have no visible evidence of having earned the title. Some of these people may indeed be helpful, but you have little recourse should they prove disreputable.

Being depressed or distraught, you're probably not in a position to comparison-shop for a therapist. I suggest that you find a comprehensive mental health clinic (one that offers a variety of services) and ask for an appointment. Often the intake worker (the first person you speak with at length) is not the one who will continue to handle your case. You can always request someone else if you wish. Most important, you will want to know that the people you see are *licensed*, not only for your own peace of mind but also because insurance companies will not as a rule reimburse you for services of unlicensed counselors.

Second, you need to consider the cost, particularly if you *don't* have insurance.

It's not as significant what kind of therapist you see as it is whether you are comfortable with the person (which doesn't mean you have to like the person all the time either).

I spent several months struggling over divorce issues with my first therapist. I *hated* going to therapy and always felt great relief when I emerged from the weekly sessions. I thought up ingenious ways to miss appointments (and I'm not going to share them with you...). Finally it dawned on me that I couldn't relate to this woman, and I might do better with someone else. All we seemed to do was fight over my desire to be in therapy, and my reasons for seeking therapy in the first place had taken a back seat.

You might also consider how available the person can be. If you find yourself seeing someone who is in town only once every two weeks, you'll be doing a lot of work on your own.

You don't have to like your therapist. The important thing is that you listen and he or she listens—that you *respect* each other.

Working through painful issues is difficult, not usually enjoyable. In other words, you're not supposed to come away feeling as if everything has been resolved in one session or two. Often it takes months or more of steady work—days of feeling that you've made a step forward, followed by days when you've fallen two steps back. It evens out in the end if you don't give up too quickly. My experience has been that young people (or anyone, for that matter) give up when the sessions become painful. Then they are left with the lingering taste of despair, and nothing further is resolved. I'll repeat: *Therapy is hard work.*

Don't feel that you have to find a person who has been through the same problems you have. A doctor doesn't have to shoot himself in the leg to understand a gunshot wound and be able to treat it. Any therapist has his or her own well of pain to draw upon in helping you deal with yours.

Realize, too, that not all therapists get along equally well with everyone. Your best friend may suggest a woman she sees as the kindest person in the world. You may see her as a badgering mean-spirited old woman. No matter. Talk to the badgering, mean-spirited, old woman and tell her you think you two have a problem. Then you both can work out whether you need someone else as a therapist or you're just using personalities as a way of getting around treatment.

I once had a client who told me at the end of our hour that I was the best therapist she'd ever had, that I had helped her so much she would be eternally grateful. While I was patting myself on the back (something I should have been too wise to do), my next client marched in for her appointment. She informed me that if I didn't get my act together and *soon*, she'd have to quit seeing me. My ego came crashing back to earth...

What can you expect therapy to do for you? First of all, you may initially feel relieved that you've found someone with whom to work on your depression. But therapy is a complicated process whereby you usually get better only by first getting worse. That sounds contradictory, but it really isn't. Sifting through the bad things in your life, you're likely to become more depressed until (with the therapist's help) you find your way out of the mess. Even a well-credentialed therapist is no guarantee that you'll get better. A psychologist once told me that if you sat a client in a therapist's office and the two of them simply read the phone book together, chances are the client would improve. That's because people often *feel* better when they have someone with whom to share their problems. Nonetheless you should come to feel you have greater control over your emotions and life; if that isn't happening, reexamine what propelled you into counseling in the first place. Sometimes it's hard to realize that you *are* better.

Certain things are unethical in treatment. A reputable therapist will never initiate sex with you. Nor will he or she accept your sexual advances, should you make any. If your therapist cannot maintain this boundary with you, *get out of treatment and report it*. Sex between client and therapist is not meant to happen. Why?

Because in the long run it will only hurt you, confuse you, and make you dependent on the therapist in an unhealthy way. The reputable therapist knows this. That doesn't mean you won't be sexually attracted to your therapist; that may very well happen. It simply means that he or she is bound by ethics *not* to act on sexual feelings.

Last of all, realize that it's not a measure of your character if you need to see someone to help you through a crisis. Sometimes it requires more strength to seek help than it does to bury the problem.

There are plenty of people out there who can help you. It's mostly a matter of finding someone you are comfortable with, someone who is reputable and ethical and willing to listen.

And like all humans, some have better days than others . . .

CHAPTER ◇ 11

Losses

Accompanying

Motherhood

I can't remember exactly how old I was when I first realized that I wasn't the center of attention in my family anymore. The limelight left me gradually, as I recall. After a while I couldn't get anywhere just by flashing my dimples. I think I stopped being cute around the time my younger brother made his entrance into the world. After Mark was born, I was supposed to be satisfied with being the big sister. Some trade-off. I don't know about you, but I never got much out of being older except more responsibility. And I sure got away with less. To this day, I remember when that same baby brother ran out the front door, down the walk, and right into the street. Who got punished for leading our parents on a merry chase down the center of the highway? I did, of course, because I was the one who had not spotted Mark climbing over the barricade in the front door. Mark was still the center of attention, and I got sent to bed early!

Age and size can have their disadvantages.

Hard to believe, but motherhood too involves growing up and losing the limelight. Other losses too. For one thing, many pregnant teenagers lose their chance to create a better life for themselves. Perhaps having struggled in a household where an assortment of adults (parents, stepparents) brought them up, some teenagers may have hoped they could make a more stable life for themselves. But instead of using their education or a job as the means to propel themselves beyond the home, they chose boyfriends and motherhood.

Given that teenage motherhood is so difficult, girls more often than not lose their chance ever to improve their circumstances. In no time they have a baby to care for and a husband to depend on. If there's no husband, they're either more entrenched in their family of origin, or they turn to welfare, which at best is only a subsistence way of living. Motherhood, under these circumstances, will bring additional hardship and lost opportunities.

Motherhood also means a loss of control over certain parts of your life. First, during the pregnancy you realize that your body is no longer your own, your emotions are out of control, and even your body does its own thing in the final stages of labor. In all stages of labor, for that matter. After delivery, everything you do is subordinated to this baby who has taken over your life. Certainly being tied down to a child who is totally dependent on you points up how out-of-control your life has become.

One of the most startling discoveries you make is that now you are responsible for another human being. Whereas you may have been the center of attention during the pregnancy, the baby now—and forever more—takes center stage. It's worse than simply growing up, because not only are you out of the limelight, but you've become one of those eternally misunderstood creatures—a mother. Remember what you thought of your own?

I can't remember just when it dawned on me that my innocent little baby would one day consider me as antiquated as my own parents seemed to me. Somehow, after pregnancy, I had become one of "them." I had to be serious and responsible. I had to worry about paying the bills on time, or just paying them period. I had to make a will and name a guardian for my child. I had to prepare three meals a day even when I didn't feel like eating anything more than a salad. After all, I was a mother now, and there was this baby depending on me to behave like one.

Like any major life event, motherhood brings with it trade-offs. Good things, like the joy of raising another human being and the opportunity to give and receive love. But there are losses too, and if you don't at least recognize them, you risk building up years of anger and resentment.

I'm talking about losses that are hard to see. The loss of your own childhood, the loss of your independence and sense of control over your life, and the loss of freedom and sometimes choices.

The most profound joy—that of loving another human being—is also the most frightening. The day my infant daughter was hospitalized for a severe case of jaundice, and the nurse took her out of my arms, I felt my insides plunge to my feet. I thought I would die if something happened to her. Suddenly I had a picture of my own parents waving good-bye to me as I flew off to Oklahoma so many years earlier.

"How did they ever let me go?" I wondered, when I was

having this much trouble just handing my baby over to the nurse. The burden of caring so much for another human being crashed onto my shoulders.

You, as teenagers, are just past being children yourselves. How much more you have given up by cutting your own childhood short to become parents.

To recognize what you've lost means also to know what you've gained. In the end, I hope you'll be able to say it was a fair trade-off.

Growing up did have a few rewards, now that I think back on it. Like later curfews and a boyfriend who wouldn't have been impressed by my baby brother in the least...

PART · IV

PARENTHOOD READY OR NOT

CHAPTER ◇ 12

Preparing
for the Baby

In this section I'm going to look at what happens once you've become a parent. Of course, that means taking you from the last idealistic days of your pregnancy right up through delivery when reality—and pain—start to sink in.

I've always wanted to teach a course on the harsh realities of parenting, because adolescents seem to have such idealistic and glamorous pictures of young married life—as if it's always full of love and sex—and only incidentally—babies.

If you feel overwhelmed by the responsibilities of parenthood, don't despair. We all were first-time parents once in our lives, and we all felt overwhelmed at some point. You can call the Visiting Nurse Association (1-800-426-2547) for referrals in your community. A visiting nurse can help show you the ropes and assess any other services you might need. It is NOT their intent to take the baby from you.

I got the shock of my life when I had my first child. I thought babies were fragile, docile creatures that slept all the time. It never occurred to me that a baby *could* stay awake all night.

If you think I'm painting an extreme picture of parenthood, you're in for a hard first year. I thought it was better for you to know some of this stuff now while you still have the opportunity to take a nap afterward. Or go to a movie. Or play the stereo full blast . . .

Before we look at how hard it might be to raise that adorable little offspring of yours, let's look at how much it's going to cost to deck him out. Have you considered what you're going to need, and have you checked out those classy baby stores? You'll need to buy a ton of baby things, but they don't have to be the most expensive.

The hospital will not let you walk out the door with your baby until they've seen that you have an approved car seat. So that will be one of your first considerations. Check out a car seat that is easy to get an infant in and out of as well as secure. If the car seat turns out to be cumbersome to use, you'll find yourself using it less and less. Your baby's safety relies on this seat, but buckling her in correctly is in your hands. Choose a car seat that doesn't have twenty different sets of harnesses, and get used to buckling it each and every ride.

You'll also need baby clothes and a lot of them unless you want to be a slave to the washing machine. Daily trips to do laundry can drain whatever energy you restore from a half night's sleep. My mother argues for drawstring nightgowns over sleepers, simply because they're easier to change a baby out of. In those first few days it will seem as if you're always changing the baby, and if your baby is a boy it may surprise you how he can soak his T-shirt through without hitting his diaper. I may be wrong, but I don't think it matters what brand of clothes you buy. You buy what you can afford, realizing of course that the baby will outgrow his or her clothes about six times that first year. Depending on the season, you might even get away with just shirts and diapers. Let your mother or grandmother buy that expensive little sailor suit or dress. You'll need your money for more practical things.

Such as a crib. There's no law that says you have to have a brass crib or one of those fancy white-painted jobs. Remember, the baby cares less about being in a designer crib than being in a loving home. You and your friends will notice the setting; the baby won't.

As if a crib isn't expensive enough, you have to buy bedding and at least a couple of extra sheets and pads. Little as it is, a baby can soak through sheets and mattress pads in no time flat. You'll need a pile of receiving blankets; again, a baby boy can soak a blanket without ever touching his diaper.

You'll also need a high chair (although some people use a baby walker alternately as a feeding station) and perhaps a stroller. You need a place to store the baby's clothing, and maybe a swing to get him or her to sleep when all else fails. You can skip the swing, of course; your mother would do just as well.

Have you priced diapers? They aren't cheap anymore, partly because they're the new designer item. Some people must think that the more colorful and heavily padded diapers are, the more effective. Other people say that you don't want a diaper to be *too* absorbent because the baby will end up staying longer in a soaked diaper before you notice. Wet diapers breed bacteria.

There's certainly nothing wrong in buying blue LUVS for boys or pink LUVS for girls, but it's not necessary, and it does get expensive. Ultimately, you should just pick the diapers you can live with; after all, you'll probably be living with them for a long time.

Baby formula costs a lot of money, and this, along with medical care, is one area where you can't skimp. Women have made deadly errors by trying to water down formula to make it last longer. Using too much water dilutes the mixture, destroying some of its nutritive value. Your baby's health will suffer. Some have been known to starve to death on watered-down formula. *Don't shortchange your baby here.*

The same goes for medical care. You cannot skip appointments simply because you think the baby is doing fine. He or she needs certain inoculations, as well as weight checks to judge growth. If you can't afford medical care, special "well baby" clinics associated with state agencies provide health care at very low cost. I cannot stress this enough. Babies can languish and sometimes contract deadly diseases later in life because parents have not been diligent with medical appointments. Healthy babies stay healthy by continuing to see doctors.

It's fun to buy baby toys because it's fun to relive the childhood you've just cut short. Most of the toys, though, are more fun for the adults at this stage. In the beginning, a baby likes human faces, bright colors, and most of all, his mother's voice. It's immaterial whether he's got Big Bird in bed with him. Even before he gets to the stage where he likes that stuffed animal, he will cherish the box it came in much more. So if you have to skimp somewhere, do it on toys right now. That doesn't mean make the nursery a sterile environment. It just means, use the money you would have spent on the Dakin $220 giraffe to buy a playpen instead.

It's hard enough to buy all the things you need if you're both working and have saved up for the baby. But if you're a teenager with little time to save and little family support, you can find yourself in over your head. There are alternatives, though. First of all, you must balance your wants and your needs. Looked at that way, you can see that some of the "must-haves" for the baby are really things you just "want" to have. The baby can do fine without designer infant jeans. He will *not* do fine without a car seat and diapers and medical care. First things first.

It may help to make up a list of things under the headings NEEDS and WANTS. Write down everything you can think of under each heading. Your "needs" list may wind up longer than your budget, but don't worry about that yet. Once you're finished, put away the "wants" list temporarily, and concentrate on the "needs" list.

If you're dependent on welfare assistance, you'll find a lot of the items out of reach. AFDC payments do not make for a cushy way of living, no matter what taxpayers like to believe.

Of your major needs, see which ones you can borrow from friends. Sometimes you can find good used furniture at garage sales or second-hand baby stores. Often these stores are run by mothers looking for a way to bring in added income without taking a regular job. They cull their attics and their friends' attics for retired baby items to sell at reduced prices. You can find some wonderful bargains without sacrificing your standards.

If you know ahead of time that you are going to be given a baby shower, let your friends know what you still need. If friends ask you point-blank what you want, don't hem and haw; *specify* what you need.

Sometimes you can combine your needs and use one item for two purposes, like a baby walker serving also as a high chair or a car seat doubling as a baby carrier. With a little thought, you can eliminate some of your needs until such time as you can afford separate items. A recent innovation is a padded insert you can buy that fits into a child carseat, making the carseat better fit an infant. The padding, which costs less than $10, keeps you from having to buy two carseats: one for the infant, and another bigger one for the toddler he'll become.

Sometimes you'll have to decide what you can do without. It used to make me angry that I couldn't afford to buy massive stuffed animals for my kids when they were born. I don't know what they'd have done with these huge creatures parked in the corners of their rooms, but it seemed unfair all the same.

Incidentally, people have become more careful about using baby walkers in the last couple of years. Many think that they can be dangerous because babies have been known to topple over in them, severely injuring themselves. The danger apparently stems from parents using the walkers as baby-sitters. Unsuspecting parents stick the baby in his walker and then go about their chores, or take a quick nap. Meanwhile, the baby kicks his little legs and shoots around the room, crashing into things he can't avoid and occasionally knocking the whole thing over—on his head. If you're going to use a walker, stay around to monitor the baby's navigation.

Growing up means learning to live with your priorities and learning to do without. More than half the baby stuff you see on TV is what advertisers want us to *think* we need. Babies don't notice the labels on their sweaters and jackets. All they care about is being warm and loved, and *that* should be your priority now.

CHAPTER 13

Delivery

I n this chapter we'll look at what happens to you emotionally as well as physically during labor and delivery. Some teenagers forget that this last part is the whole point of pregnancy. Small wonder; it's the hardest part.

Before I say anything about labor itself, let me remind you of one thing: Everyone experiences labor and delivery differently because humans vary in their capacity to tolerate pain and stress. For some women I've talked with, labor has been no worse than severe menstrual cramps. For others, it has been much more agonizing. I had always heard that labor was like having bad cramps. You can imagine how cheated I felt when I realized that mine was a whole lot worse than that. So, in the name of fairness, I'm going to paint as many different views of the childbirth experience as I've come across. Perhaps you will find something among the stories that you can relate to.

When Bonnie was in labor, she remembers the surprising ache in her back, of all places. "No one ever told me my back was going to hurt," she said. "I wasn't even so sure the baby wasn't going to come out my ass."

Bonnie was stretching the point a little, though she really was in the dark as to just what childbirth would be like. Oh, she knew that the baby would exit the vaginal canal, but I'm not so sure she understood what was causing the pain. Since her cervix had to stretch open to 10 centimeters to accommodate the baby's head and shoulders, her pain came from the cervix stretching open and each contraction of the uterus. Some people feel the contractions in the back rather than the abdomen. If you have a weak back, you'll probably be one of them. Because I had been accustomed to having menstrual cramps every month, I figured I could handle the slightly more intense abdominal pains of labor. The back pains, though, were much harder to handle because I wasn't used to it. Even with the nurse constantly massaging my lower back.

Another teenager, Karen, complained that the whole experience hurt so much she never wanted to have another baby. Not only did she have an unusually long labor (thirty-six hours), but she had had nine months of scare stories from well-meaning friends.

When I spoke with nurses about teenagers in the delivery room, they all mentioned how unprepared the girls were for the pain of childbirth. Even girls who had taken Lamaze classes and supposedly knew what the experience would be like were still shocked at the *amount* of pain they felt. They often kept asking for pain medication even when they had had the maximum allowed.

This is as good a place as any to suggest checking out the various options for pain relief in labor. These are things you should talk over with your doctor in advance, in case he knows a reason why a certain medicine cannot be used in your case.

Another word of caution: Demerol, supposedly a potent pain reliever, doesn't always take away the pain of contractions. From my own experience, Demerol merely fogs the brain so that you're not sure whether you're dreaming or dead. But the pain still seeps through...

Some medications are more painful in being *administered* than the pain itself. Some shots are not even effective until long after you've passed the most painful stage of labor.

I'm not sure why teenagers say they feel so much more pain during labor; perhaps it is because their bodies are not yet ready to handle childbirth. Perhaps, too, it reflects the younger person's intolerance for discomfort. Adults are usually more socialized to bear pain and keep quiet about it.

This in no way means that all of you will have difficult birth experiences. Because I didn't want you tricked by the idea of simple menstrual-type cramps, I've told the hard cases first. But there are girls who have delivered babies at home, not even realizing they were pregnant. And I had one friend who finally decided to see her doctor because her mild contractions were so closely spaced, only to discover that she was fully dilated and ready to deliver. You can always hope that you're going to be one of these girls.

Teenagers complained to me not so much about the aches and pains of childbirth but about the nurses who helped them. If they grew accustomed to a certain nurse and her style, they often felt confused and abandoned when the shift changed and that nurse went off duty. Girls seemed to depend more on their nurse than on their mother or partner. If the nurse had a prickly personality, the whole experience became more stressful for the teenage mother, which made the contractions more intense. (You're supposed to remain relaxed during labor, so the pain will be less. It's a tall order to stay relaxed during a painful contraction. Believe me, it's the last thing you feel like doing!) If the teenagers sensed their nurse to be more supportive than critical, they were more apt to follow breathing instructions and cooperate in the birth.

What about the girls' mothers? Nurses told me they were surprised at the number of mothers who came to the hospital with their daughters. Often these mothers reversed their whole relationship with their daughters, some of whom might have previously been kicked out of the household. Sometimes after delivery these same mothers forgot the past and took their daughter and grandchild home to help with postpartum care.

I can only speak for myself, but childbirth is not an experience I would have wanted to go through alone. It doesn't have to be your mother accompanying you into the delivery room; it can be your husband, your boyfriend, your sister, or your next-door neighbor. Hospital staffs aren't usually judgmental about your support person; what they care about is that someone is there with you, because a support person can make the experience a whole lot easier. He or she can calm and placate you when you've had your fill of labor; he or she can encourage you when you're ready to quit; and he or she can indulge you when you're looking for someone to scream at.

Terry went through labor with her whole family on hand. Her mother and aunt and sister all stayed during labor and even through the delivery. At first it was interesting to have so many people around, but as the time dragged on and Terry became increasingly uncomfortable, her family members became more of a distraction. Terry resented their excitement about the impending birth; she felt as if she were going through hell while they were sitting around chatting. Terry told me later that she had wished her mother had given her more attention during that time, but my hunch is that no matter what her mother would have done, there comes a point in labor when the pain is so intense that it doesn't matter what anyone else does. What any laboring woman really wants at that point is for the pain to end.

One word of advice: If you plan to have more than one person with you in the labor room, make sure ahead of time that the support people realize they are there for *you*, not to enjoy each other's company. If in the end they are distracting you rather than supporting you, feel free to ask them to leave. You need your energy for the birth, not to compete for your friends' attention.

Allison's mother accompanied her to labor and stayed through delivery, but right in the middle of the process, Allison's boyfriend showed up. Unfortunately, he didn't know how irritable a woman can be in the last stages of labor. When he asked Allison if she'd like him to stay, she replied through clenched teeth, "I don't care *what* you do."

Allison really didn't have anything against her boyfriend, who had not gone through Lamaze classes with her because of his work schedule. However, when she said she didn't care what he did, he figured she didn't want him around, so he kissed her good-bye and went to sit in the waiting room. Allison was then a little miffed that he hadn't understood what she was really saying: "I'm too wrapped up in pain to decide anything right now. You do what you're comfortable with."

Labor can be a deceiving proposition. At first when the doctor tells you this is the real thing, you may think, "Well, this isn't so bad." I remember my own first time, sitting on the couch at the birth center and thinking to myself, "Well, if this is as bad as it gets, it's a piece of cake!"

A few hours later the cramps moved around to my back

and the pain got harder. "I must be fully dilated now," I said to the nurse, "because it's starting to get uncomfortable." (What an understatement!)

The nurse checked and said, "You're only 6 centimeters. You're not there yet."

Well, when all you're interested in hearing is that you're 10 centimeters dilated, hearing that you're only 6 is grounds for killing the nurse. By the time I hit 8 centimeters, I had already told my husband that was enough for the day and would he please take me home. (Although I knew there was no way on earth I could stand up at that point and walk out the door.) By the time I hit 10 centimeters, I had not only sworn off having another kid, I'd sworn off doing *anything* that would land me in this predicament again.

But then our daughter was finally born, and the pain disappeared instantly. It was almost as if there had never been any pain to begin with; it had been replaced with a tremendous burst of energy. (Not all births have to be painful, remember. Mine was unmedicated that first time; there are far easier routes, which I opted for the next few times around.)

Terry told me she also felt "elated" after birth. "And," she said, "if I could skip the pain part, I'd do it all over again. I thought it was great."

It's hard work getting the baby, but most people I've talked with agree it was well worth it. The support people helping the teenager through the birth experience report an increased bonding with the baby and its mother.

"I have other nieces and nephews," one woman said to me, "but I helped this one come into the world. This one is special."

Not all births are vaginal deliveries. Sometimes you wind up having a caesarean section, in which the doctor takes the baby out through an incision he makes in your abdomen. (Don't worry; you'll have plenty of anesthesia for that. It's major surgery.) After a caesarean you may experience some let-down if you had wanted to have the baby "the usual way." But the main thing is to have a baby safely; keep that in mind instead.

There are some different physical sensations after a caesarean: the sting of the incision, the lethargy. You have to remember you've just had major surgery; your recovery will be slower than after a vaginal delivery.

After Sandy's caesarean she was afraid to stand up. "I knew I'd been cut open less than twenty-four hours earlier," she said. "I thought my insides might fall out when I stood up." (Don't worry; the doctor knew what he was doing. Your insides are fully intact. It just hurts like fire when you first stand up.)

For fathers, a wife's caesarean, especially an unanticipated one, can be a frightening experience. Josh was ushered out of his wife's labor room when the doctor discovered that the baby's heart rate had gone down. The doctor decided to do emergency surgery and deliver the baby immediately. Because he would give Josh's wife general anesthesia, he did not want Josh present during the surgery. Unfortunately, Josh interpreted his quick ousting as a sign that something had gone wrong and more danger was yet to come. Ten minutes later when the doctor came out to tell Josh he had a fine, healthy son, Josh was relieved. But when the doctor left without mentioning how his wife had fared, Josh figured she must have died or something during the surgery and the doctor hadn't known how to tell him. By the time he was reunited with his healthy wife, he was almost beside himself with fear.

Some girls react to their newborn with fascination, confusion, adoration, and disgust. Yes, I said disgust. Bonnie told me she watched the whole process of birth in the overhead mirrors, but once the baby was out and the doctor placed the bloody newborn on her belly, she recoiled in disgust.

"That was gross," she later told me.

"But you watched the whole bloody birth," I said.

"That part was fascinating," Bonnie said. "But I didn't want a bloody baby on my belly."

Terry was confused when they handed her her baby. "What am I supposed to do with her?" she wondered.

Karen had a different experience when she first saw her baby. "She was so purple, and the cord was wrapped around her," she told me. "I was scared for the baby." When Karen had determined that the baby was fine, she said, "I felt like crying. Everything was over."

Just as you can have different kinds of labor experiences, you can also respond in different ways in the afterglow of the birth. Some girls feel a burst of pride—partly because they've created this new life, partly because they have survived the ordeal. There's a period afterward of "falling in love" when bonding occurs or is strengthened if it has occurred before birth.

A nurse working in the newborn nursery told me about a time when she was sitting rocking a crying infant. Hilary, age fifteen, had just delivered a baby girl, and she came into the nursery. Hilary's baby was on the other side of the room sleeping, and Hilary watched the nurse who so ably quieted this infant.

"My baby is the quiet one over there," Hilary said.

The nurse had calmed the infant she was holding and was tucking it back into its bed. Hilary marveled at her ease with infants.

"Aren't they all so sweet?" she said. "I can't wait to have another one."

What the nurse tried to tell Hilary, who was only half-listening, was that some of those babies were sweet only because they were getting round-the-clock care by shifts of nurses.

"Your baby wasn't so sweet and quiet an hour ago," she said.

Sometimes the lull of those first days in the hospital is really the calm before the storm. It's alarming to bring home that adorable little infant from the nursery and discover that she doesn't sleep through the night. And worse: to discover that there isn't a nurse around to take over when you just can't take another crying jag.

A few words about bonding. You may have heard that women feel this great maternal gush at childbirth—an overwhelming feeling of love for the child. That probably does happen with some people, but it doesn't always happen exactly that way, and it doesn't always happen period. When my own daughter was born, I was so re-lieved that the pain had ended that I didn't notice I hadn't experienced any maternal flood of emotion. When my husband and I took her home I expected to feel something maternal, but I didn't. After a while I interpreted my lack of "bonding" as a sign that I was a "bad" mother. Mothers are supposed to be attached to their kids, and the fact that I didn't feel anything beyond a mild fondness was proof to me that I was unfit.

A few days later when my daughter was hospitalized for jaundice, I thought I would die without her. As the nurse took her out of my arms and I gazed at her from behind the glass, I realized that I had indeed bonded with her and that was why I was missing her so painfully right then. Some-how outside of my awareness, I had bonded after all. It hadn't come through any great outpouring of emotion; it was just a slow process of falling in love.

Be careful when you compare yourself to other mothers. If you don't find yourself as maternal as you think you should be (whatever that is), realize that this is a situation in which you have to learn as you go. Everyone has a different way of expressing herself, and most of the time we mesh just fine with our babies. There are such things as personality clashes, and sometimes it is hard to bond with a baby who has a temperamental disposition, or who is very different from us. Let yourself love the baby in your own way and time. Have a trusted adult friend on hand to show you the ropes if need be.

Some teenagers are nervous about taking their baby home that first time, whereas others who have grown up caring for young kids feel no special qualms at all. It will be challenging enough around your house in the next few weeks. If you have someone to help you through the first awkward moments, you're one step ahead of the game.

THE FATHER'S PERSPECTIVE

I haven't forgotten that guys go through this whole process too, whether they spend the time in the labor and delivery rooms or wait it out in a different part of the hospital. Guys have mentioned feeling fascinated and overwhelmed at the experience of birth, especially that moment when a fuzzy little head first appears. I've rarely had a woman tell me she cried at birth, but several guys have told me they did. It is a moment unlike anything else you'll ever experience, seeing your own child born. For most, it is an incredibly bonding event, solidifying all the more your relationship with its mother.

Not all the guys react with fascination, though, as much as they expect to. Some get queasy seeing their wife's discomfort, and when it starts to get bloody their knees start to give way. If you're faint of heart, decide whether you're going to be more of a hindrance than a help. I've always encouraged guys to be optimistic; they might come through when they least expect it. And if their legs turn to jelly, the nurses will get them out of the way so that the "show can go on."

For the guys in the waiting room, I can only guess that they're filled with equal amounts of curiosity and anxiety. Sometimes it's worse wondering what's going on than it is watching.

WHEN YOU GET HOME

Childbirth is said to be the most painful event a woman can go through. That's certainly debatable; I think *raising* the child can be almost as painful. (Just ask your parents.)

You can do some things, though, to lessen the trauma. First of all, if you're confused about how to handle a newborn, how to bathe it or feed it, don't stew in your embarrassment. There are plenty of nurses around only too willing to impart some of their wisdom to you. They can also arrange for a visiting health nurse to look in on you at home and see that you're doing okay. (A standard practice at one hospital is to arrange a visiting health nurse for all teenagers who give birth there. Karen was angry and embarrassed when the nurse showed up on her doorstep, because she thought the hospital assumed she couldn't care for her baby. That had not been the case.) Actually it is to your advantage that someone is interested enough to look *you* up rather than wait for you to make the call yourself.

You can also call on your old Lamaze friends, who now are first-time parents too. Sometimes it's easier to struggle through motherhood learning things together, and at other times it's worse than the blind leading the blind.

If after your delivery you find yourself increasingly depressed, talk to your doctor. Sometimes it's a matter of trying to shoulder too much responsibility at once. Perhaps another adult or your husband could take over more of the care so that you have time for yourself. If your depression doesn't respond to vacations and rewards, however, you may have a hormonal disturbance that can lead to true postpartum depression. In this condition it's not a matter of willing yourself out of the dumps. You need prompt medical attention and someone to take over much of the baby's care. Your energy will be needed in your own recovery.

Some people think they have to raise the baby in isolation, as if the task of mothering were so monumental that it can only be done by focusing all your energy on it, leaving nothing for a life beyond that.

Believe me, this is no time to isolate yourself. Maintain your old friendships if you can. Find others who are in similar circumstances and share ideas or baby-sitters.

Just because you did not have a nurturing family does not mean that you can't learn about nurturing from someone else. Sometimes girls who have a loving adult friend can use her as a role model, salvaging years of their own emotional neglect. Remember, you can't give something to your child that you've never had or known. Part of parenting is sharing early lessons of love. If you had few close moments with your own parents, seek out other people with whom you might be able to get that kind of feedback. You can't undo your past, but you can enhance what you have now. Raising kids doesn't simply mean feeding and clothing them. It especially means *nurturing* them.

And last, probably my best piece of advice. RELAX. Everyone has been a first-time mother once in her life...

CHAPTER 14

Reality Replaces
the Fantasy Child

T his will be the chapter where you think, "My gosh, what have I gotten myself into?" because I'm not going to tell you how glamorous motherhood is or how soon you should contemplate adding to your new family. In fact, if I tell you enough stories about my own experiences, I should make you wonder whose crazy idea it was to chance a pregnancy in the first place.

In some schools the Home Economics department has a program in which the teenagers become adoptive mothers of dolls for a week. The girls carry the dolls with them everywhere, and if they want a few moments without the doll, they have to arrange a baby-sitter, just as if the doll were a real baby. The idea is to give the teenager the feeling of caring for an infant on a twenty-four-hour basis. Usually by the end of the program the teenagers are relieved to turn in their dolls and regain their freedom. It's a harmless lesson in the rigors of parenting. Maybe if every school adopted the program, fewer teenagers would risk pregnancy.

When I was a teenager growing up in Maine, I thought having a baby was a grown-up thing to do too. Not only grown-up, but sexy as well. Sexy, because obviously it entailed doing something sexual to get one in the first place. There was one fleeting period of time when I would gladly have traded my last several years as a teenager to be grown-up and pregnant.

Today's teenager may be encouraged to have a career, but at the same time the media also encourage her to entice everything in pants from here to Kalamazoo. It's hard to be serious about a career and be a sexpot too. The media even hype the glamor of unwed pregnancy by focusing on people like Jessica Lange and the television character Murphy Brown, neither of whom married the father of their child. The struggle against the desire to have your boyfriend's baby is made more difficult by these role models.

Remember when I spoke earlier about that fantasy child? Everyone has an idea about what his or her offspring will look and act like. It's always in positive terms, too. (I've never heard anyone bragging that her baby-to-be will turn out a hell-raiser who keeps her up nights.) No, people always think in glowing terms of the baby growing inside them. Think back on what you were expecting. A spitting image of your boyfriend or husband? A little girl just like you—someone to doll up in frilly dresses? Did you imagine too that this little infant would sleep most of the day while you and your husband/boyfriend cavorted the time away?

Here's reality...

More often than not the baby is cranky, maybe partly because he senses that you're nervous and unsure of yourself. In any event, he only settles down when your aunt who has raised six of her own comes to visit you. He falls asleep in *her* arms, but manages to stay awake for eight-hour stretches when you're alone and dying for a nap. You're too nervous to breast-feed him, and he spits up the formula. You take him to the doctor's, and the people in the waiting room say, "Oh, is that your little *brother?*"

And when you get in to see the doctor, he sighs because he probably thinks you're young and incompetent, and all you want to do is get out of there as fast as you can. You suspect he's noting in his chart that you're an unfit mother because you haven't been able to clear up the baby's diaper rash yet, and the next thing you know he'll be sending a social worker to your door to investigate the situation.

Well, RELAX. Reality isn't that bad, although teenagers can get carried away with their lack of confidence and their fear that someone is watching their every step (or misstep, as the case may be.)

But reality is certainly sleepless nights for a while unless someone (your mother?) gets up nights to care for the hungry infant. Most newborns cannot eat enough at one time to stay satisfied for more than four-hour stretches. Hence, they wake you up for 4 a.m. feedings. You may be one of those people who can get up in the middle of the night, feed and change the baby (always do it in that order too or you'll be changing him twice), and then fall right back to sleep. Most people, though, can't do that. If the baby has a 2 a.m. feeding and then a 5 or 6 a.m. feeding, you'll be one of the walking dead in no time at all.

Do you ever wonder who invented the methods of sleep torture in POW camps? Obviously someone who knew a lot about mothers. Interrupting your night's sleep can eventually make you psychotic. Before you get to that point, however, you'll just be edgy and irritable, with the clouded judgment of someone fighting a hangover. I'm not exagger-

ating about the craziness that comes from sleep depriva-
tion. My own first child refused to sleep for more than half
an hour a day. The only time she was quiet was when
someone carried her around in a snugli, or she was riding
in the car, or the vacuum cleaner was roaring underneath
her crib. I ended up driving around the countryside at all
hours of the night because I couldn't stand to hear her fuss.
Sometimes when I couldn't bear one more moment of
wakefulness, I'd turn on the vacuum cleaner, stash it by
her crib, and lie down for a while. I thought I was going to
lose my mind during those times.

Having a cranky baby can cause chaos in other ways. Not
only will she disrupt your sleep to the point where you
don't know whether you've just gone to bed or are just
waking up, but she'll undermine your self-confidence.
You'll start asking yourself, "Why am I such a lousy
mother? Why can't I calm her down?" (It's hard not to take
that kind of behavior personally.)

It's important, though, that you're attentive to your
newborn, because an infant can get seriously ill so quickly.
It doesn't require constant vigilance, but it does mean
attention. It might be useful to take some parenting classes
at your local hospital or through the YWCA. Even if you're
living at home and your parents are helping out with the
baby, you need to know the basics of child care and what to
do in an emergency. Sometimes child-care books are especially helpful, because you can return to them over and
over again to look up things you're unsure of.

If you're one of the lucky ones who have a placid baby or
one who sleeps through the night from the moment you
bring her home, I don't want to hear about it. I prefer to
believe those babies are figments of your imagination; they
don't really exist.

There's nothing especially glamorous about changing

messy diapers. Pretty soon your whole world revolves around whether Junior had a bowel movement today or not, and it's no wonder friends forget to include you in get-togethers after a while. They either assume you wouldn't join them in the first place, or worse: that you'd bring the "kid" with you. Just wait until the first time you go to hand someone something and realize your hand smells of baby diarrhea!

If there's any time left over for your husband or boyfriend, it will not be quality time. My experience has been that the baby gets all the quality time, and what's left belongs to you and your husband. But usually before your husband gets even that time, you've fallen asleep. Remember that I said motherhood wasn't really sexy? Well, sometimes mothers are not very sexy creatures; they're so wrapped up in being mothers that they can't shift gears and be wives or lovers anymore.

I wasn't a very good wife. At least, not with the first baby. I *wanted* to connect with my husband in a loving, nonmaternal way. It's just that I wasn't *looking* very nonmaternal those first few weeks. Dripping breasts, a lumpy body, the smells of baby all over me, including the lingering scent of dirty diapers. I mean, how could anyone get very romantic over me?

Not that there's much time for you and your husband to fight for; but sometimes it gets to be too big a strain to spend it nurturing the guy as well as the baby. Some men become outright jealous of the infant—even their own spitting image. Believe me, the last thing a woman wants is another baby to take care of.

For guys, the experience of fatherhood seems to be a shock. Their ability to throw themselves into the experience seems related to the degree of commitment they feel to their new family and their own level of maturity. For some of you, the pile of smelly diapers will simply over-whelm you. Babies aren't always cute and smelling of baby powder. Single guys who are visiting fathers may be disen-chanted with their girlfriend's preoccupation with the baby. It's hard to admit to competing with a baby for your girl's attention; it's probably easier to fade away from the relationship.

Not to shortchange you guys who are devoted fathers, some of you help out with the baby even after a full day of work or school. Usually these guys are secure in their girlfriend's/wife's love and not insistent on a clean baby all the time.

Nevertheless, I think most guys are surprised to find that fatherhood is more tedious than they were led to believe.

After all that attention lavished on you, the pregnant teenager, it's hard to play second fiddle to a baby, particu-larly a demanding, ungrateful one. Some days when people came to visit me, bearing gifts for the baby, I wanted to say, "What did you bring *me*?"

Reality is that now you're the mother and not destined to be the center of attention anymore. Even if you're blessed with a docile, happy baby, unless you have someone to help you watch the little cherub, you're going to be carting him or her everywhere with you—just as those girls car-ried their dolls with them to every class and every after-school activity. Many people love babies, but they're usually the ones who don't have to take them home at night. If you find yourself getting weighed down by all this one-to-one with your baby, find someone to baby-sit for a while before you start thinking of him or her as your "keeper." You can't leave your baby unattended just because he's asleep. That's neglect. If you want to go some-where you either cart him along or call your Mom.

The sad realities are many for married teenagers. You start wondering, "Where did the glamor go? Why am I always so tired? Why don't we have time for each other anymore? Why does it cost this much to feed a kid?"

But there are also questions for single parents. "How do I start a new relationship when I have to take the baby everywhere? Where will I find time for another person in my life? How can I attract someone when I'm so tired all the time?"

If you're overtired and overburdened with child care, as many of you will naturally be without family support, you are risking the possibility of abusing the baby. Especially so, if you grew up abused yourself. You need adequate, restful sleep in order to think straight and react calmly. If you're not getting sleep, you're setting yourself and the baby up for some explosive consequences. Seizing the baby in a sudden burst of anger, shaking him or her to stop the crying, can permanently damage the baby's spinal column and neck. It can cause internal bleeding; it can kill the baby. Just one unchecked moment of anger. Throwing the baby down hard on the mattress can shake up his insides, again causing internal bleeding. Or death. Babies are not meant to be tossed around. If you're afraid you're reaching the breaking point, call your public health nurse—if you have one—or Parents Anonymous, an abuse hotline. Seek supportive counseling to learn better ways to handle your anger. If your baby's crying is pushing the buttons on your self-control, lay the baby in his crib and go outside for a moment (not down the street or over to a neighbor's), or take a noisy, warm shower to calm your nerves. You need a break or a friend—or both.

Some of you may not think you'd ever hurt your baby,

but you still might worry that a social worker will investigate your home and accuse you of child abuse. It's frightening to think that others (the welfare department) have the power to take your child away if they believe you're abusing him or her. Usually there are good indications of abuse, but I've spoken with teenagers who swore they weren't hurting their child, although it was clear that something *was* happening to the baby. The mother accused the day-care center; the day-care center accused the mother. Some girls are afraid that their boyfriend or boyfriend's parents will find fault with their handling of the baby so that they can get custody. It's hard enough to deal with normal, everyday anxiety about bringing up a baby. It's worse when you're constantly afraid your youth will be grounds to lose your baby. It won't be, as long as you are responsible in meeting the baby's needs and are nonabusive (which means not neglectful either.)

The way a teenager responds to her baby depends on several things: her level of maturity, for one thing, because caring for a baby means putting the baby's needs before your own. It also depends on how much support she has. The girl who has her mother or an involved husband with whom to share these new responsibilities will be fresher and more rested. And of course, it depends on the baby's disposition. Some babies are simply harder to deal with than others. It has nothing to do with you personally. It's just genetics.

A FEW WORDS ABOUT PARENTS

For those of you who choose to live at home and utilize your parents' support (be it financial, emotional, or otherwise), be prepared for some trade-offs. Early on you must decide how much of a role they will play in your baby's care, and the three of you must agree on it. Are they going to act like grandparents or another set of parents?

If you abdicate your role as parent, you can't complain when they take over the role themselves. It's not fair to expect your parents to foot the bills and be the baby-sitters (while you're off with your friends) and then to squawk because they have assumed a bigger share in the child-rearing than you wanted to give them. If you accept their help, you're allowing them some say in your affairs. Getting along with your parents after you become a parent yourself is one of the most difficult tasks you'll face. Sit down ahead of time, talk about ground rules, but realize that you can't have it both ways. If you're going to be a parent, don't expect your mother or father to do more than a grandparent's share of the work.

On the other hand, if you find yourself in a constant battle with your parents over the baby's care, you may choose to live with someone else or on your own if you can afford it. It is undoubtedly more difficult managing alone, but intrusive parents who undermine your authority with your child may be equally destructive. If you spend more time fighting with them than raising the baby, it's time to reassess your need for their help.

Once the glamor of pregnancy wears off and the excitement of delivery fades, how many relationships weather the crisis of young parenthood? I have no statistics, but I have some stories. Several teenagers shared with me the state of their current relationships. Some who married as teenagers are still married today and happy too. Some wouldn't have changed a thing. Some would have waited longer to have children. Some would have waited longer to marry—maybe test other relationships first.

One of the girls who is now fifteen and has a three-month-old infant says she still sees her boyfriend (the father of the baby) even though she considers him too unreliable to marry.

"If he's so unreliable, why are you still with him?" I asked her one day.

"Well, there isn't anyone else right now," she said. "I've been with Max since I was eleven."

"So you're saying it's just a comfortable relationship," I prompted.

"I know what he's like, yes," she said.

"Does he support the baby?" I asked.

"He buys the diapers," she said.

Jill is another single teenager, age sixteen, with a six-month-old baby. She lives at home with her parents, which she says she prefers to marriage right now. Her mother, with whom she is very close, helps her with the baby, and she still sees her boyfriend daily. They had broken up before she discovered she was pregnant, but she says he wanted to be part of the experience, so they got back together. Every week they grab a cart at the grocery store and do their joint shopping for the baby. Jill says it feels kind of romantic as a couple, walking down the aisles, pulling baby juice and cereal off the shelves to pile into the cart. Her boyfriend pays for the baby food and supplies, which is the extent of his support.

"We're just like a married couple," Jill said.

"Except that when you go home at night, you go to separate houses and beds," I said.

"Well, he comes over during the day when my parents aren't home. We still have opportunities for sex," she said.

"But what I meant was, you have all the hard parts of being married—having a kid to support, and none of the good parts—getting to spend the night in each other's arms," I said.

"Well, I can't imagine not living with my mother right now," Jill said. "She's helped me so much, you know. We're not ready for marriage yet. We'll get married after I finish high school."

I have no doubt that Jill is a devoted mother; I do have my suspicions about her ability to translate this experience into a marriage in the near future. I think the two may find it was easier when they were just buying groceries together.

Although Bonnie is still married to the father of her child, she reports that she and the children are all emotionally abused by him. One of these days Bonnie may get in a position to leave him, but for now she tolerates his treatment. She believes he might change—I'm betting *she* will change first.

Aimee and Bradley are still happily married. Because of their families' support, they have made time for themselves and each other. They kept their aspirations high—Aimee may go to law school—and they both finished high school. When Aimee graduated this past year, her little daughter went with them to the ceremony, demonstrating better than words that some teenagers can beat the odds.

CHAPTER ◇ 15

Birth Control and Common Sense

Just because you're old enough to have a baby and you're taking responsibility for it doesn't mean you won't make the same mistake twice. Like getting pregnant again. People (and I'm not just referring to teenagers) forget how they wound up pregnant the first time, and before they know it they're back in the same position. Only they have a toddler to watch while they're going through this pregnancy.

If you're concerned about getting pregnant again, I suggest you read some of the excellent books available on contraception. Some good examples: *Coping with Birth Control* by Michael Benson, MD (one in this series), *A Young Woman's Guide to Sex* and *A Young Man's Guide to Sex*, both by Jay Gale, PhD. The best thing you can do for yourself is not to throw away your options. The only way to prevent future pregnancy is either to forgo sex entirely or find ways to make it safe.

It is a myth that you can't conceive again until you've

had a period. It's equally untrue that you can't get pregnant if you're nursing. Haven't you noticed in school some of the kids in the same family spaced only a year apart? How do you think that happened?

If you're unconcerned about getting pregnant again because you think your mother or grandmother will raise another baby, you're already demonstrated that you're too immature to be engaging in sex in the first place. The mature person, be she a teenager or a woman in her thirties, knows that sex implies responsibility—knowing how to protect herself not only from unplanned pregnancies but from sexually transmitted diseases (STDs) as well.

If you have been involved with a family planning clinic because of your previous pregnancy, you have probably been given contraceptive information. If you're not involved with a clinic, I suggest that you talk with your doctor about the various methods of birth control.

The most reliable methods for you at this point will be the pill, the diaphragm, the condom, and a new method called Norplant. For the first two methods and the third you will need to see a doctor; the pill requires a doctor's prescription (and a physical to determine that you have no health problems that would make the pill dangerous for you to use), and the diaphragm requires you be fitted by a doctor. (It is not enough that you use someone else's diaphragm—even your mother's or your sister's. A diaphragm must be fitted to the individual body, which means being refitted after pregnancy or a weight gain of more than ten pounds.) The Norplant must be inserted by a doctor.

As I mentioned in a previous chapter, it's not enough to buy the packets of pills and hope for the best. You must be familiar with the instructions, and you must take the pills *consistently*. If you're getting sick from them, and especially if you're vomiting, be sure to use a back-up method of birth control, because you're probably not keeping down the amount of hormone needed to prevent pregnancy. If your body still can't handle the pills after a trial period, ask your doctor for either a change in the dosage or another method of birth control. Remember, pills are almost 100 percent effective *only* when they are taken *consistently*. If you can't remember to take the pill every day, this method isn't for you.

A diaphragm is another good means of birth control because it is relatively easy to use (you insert the cup-shaped diaphragm into the vagina to cover the cervix and surrounding area). It also helps to prevent the spread of STDs and the AIDS virus when combined with spermicidal cream containing nonoxynol-9. The tricky part about the diaphragm is inserting it so that it covers the cervix properly. It is not meant to fit snugly over the cervix like the cervical cap, but if it is inserted haphazardly it can serve as a gate, ushering the sperm right into the uterus. Make sure before you leave the doctor's office that a nurse has checked to see that you can insert the diaphragm properly.

It is also important to use a spermicidal jelly with the diaphragm to increase its effectiveness. If sperm do get past the barrier of the diaphragm, the spermicide will kill them. Do not use petroleum jelly as a lubricant when using a diaphragm; an oil-based agent (such as Vaseline or baby oil) will damage the diaphragm. It will eventually leak, and you know what that means. Use KY jelly instead if you need a lubricant. Borrow it from the baby supplies in the nursery.

I hope it goes without saying that the diaphragm is only as good as the person who uses it. Inserting a diaphragm after a few seconds of intercourse is a few seconds too late. Using it only at those times of the month you believe to be unsafe is irresponsible. *No time is safe.*

Norplant is now available and is 99.5 percent effective in preventing pregnancy. You can hardly do better than that. (Unless, of course, you don't engage in sex at all.) You can read about Norplant in the advertising section of most women's magazines. Norplant consists of six matchstick-like progesterone-filled tubes that the doctor implants under the skin in your upper arm. Its effectiveness lasts for five years, at which time the doctor takes it out. Your fertility is immediately restored, unless you choose to have another implant.

The advantages: you don't have to worry about doing something every day, like take a pill. The side effects are reportedly less severe than what you experience on the pill. If the implant is properly installed (and by the way, it doesn't hurt to have the implant), you'll hardly notice that it's there. And, of course, the biggest advantage is that it's so very effective.

The disadvantages: it is an expensive system. It costs about $800 for a doctor to implant the tubes and then take them out at a later date. Many doctors do not know how to implant them, and can cause an unsightly mess in their attempts. Norplant tends to be less effective in preventing conception in women who weigh more than 150 pounds. You also will not be a candidate for the implant if you have heart problems, liver disease, diabetes, high blood pressure, or a history of breast cancer in your family. Of course, it's greatest disadvantage is that it does nothing to prevent the transmission of sexually transmitted diseases, including AIDS.

There are other methods, such as the sponge (which supposedly is not as effective for those who have had a baby) and natural birth control, involving temperature taking and mucus reading. I'm not going to discuss them, because a teenager is generally not familiar enough with her body—nor is the body regular enough—to allow for these methods to be reliable.

The other method—the condom—is not only a good contraceptive but also the best means to prevent the transmission of STDs and the AIDS virus. It's important for the male to buy condoms made of latex (because they prevent the spread of the AIDS virus better than condoms made of animal skin) and to use them before *any* contact with your partner's vagina. It's equally important when you withdraw after ejaculation not to let the condom slip off the penis. *Any contact of bodily fluids* can spread the AIDS virus if it is present. And of course, sperm can swim into the vagina and propel themselves up the fallopian tubes, even if they were deposited in a few drops at the entrance to the vagina. All it takes is one sperm and one egg to make a baby.

Spermicidal foam should also be used with condoms—but *not in the condom itself*, which it can cause to slip off. Follow the instructions that come with the package.

A word about nonoxynol-9: It is the most effective ingredient in killing sperm, but it can be abrasive, and many people are allergic to it. If you're one of them, talk to your doctor about what you can substitute.

Another thing—if you're turned off by all the fuss of inserting spermicidal foam and wearing condoms, this isn't the method for you. My experience has been that if teenagers are uncomfortable with a procedure, they won't follow it to a T. Birth control isn't a half-hearted proposition. You either do it right or it won't work; it's as simple as that. It is unarguably messy to use foam and condoms, and it requires forethought to insert your diaphragm and remember the condom. (By the way, don't carry condoms in your wallet. The heat from your body will break them down.) But if you're convinced you'll remember to use the pill, then you must be doubly sure of your partner's health. AIDS is not something that happens only to adults, gay men, and drug users. Teenagers constitute the fastest growing segment of the population with HIV infection because they are the people who least anticipate it and take precautions against it. You are always susceptible when you don't know your partner's history (whether he uses drugs or needles or has engaged in bisexual behavior), and especially if you have multiple partners yourself.

AIDS can kill you. There is no cure for it. There is no such thing as safe sex: Condoms are the best barrier against transmission, but abstinence is the only sure-fire method. I know it seems as if teenagers will live forever, but the virus causing AIDS doesn't know that. It kills indiscriminately. An unplanned pregnancy may change your life, but it won't take it. AIDS will.

Sexually transmitted diseases (STDs) can also make you ill. Not only that, but left untreated some can lead to sterility. It's hard for teenagers to consider the consequences of their behavior when the results might not show up for several years. But this is another time when you have to use common sense. STDs don't go away by themselves; they must be medically treated, and you must inform any partners so that they can also be treated. In the long run, it's better to prevent the diseases than try to minimize the damage after it has been done. (If you wind up pregnant on top of getting an STD, I don't have to tell you that that seriously complicates your delivering a healthy baby.)

*   *   *

Before you have a second child, get yourself in the best circumstances possible: a stable homelife, a secure, well-paying job, and time and energy enough to devote to another demanding baby. Remember, you're not going to be trading this first child in for the baby. You're going to have two babies at home, with twice the demands for your attention. And don't be surprised if your first child resents your ousting him from the limelight and giving it to his sibling.

Do you remember my saying at the beginning of this book that there are no such things as accidents? Well, in this last section I'm going to talk more about that, because I think it's important for you to know how you wound up pregnant the first time so you can avoid doing the same thing again. It's hard enough having a baby when you're a teenager; imagine how much more difficult it will be if you have two while you're a teenager.

Look back over the past year and think about where you were emotionally just before you got pregnant. What was your home life like? How were you doing in school? Were there any family circumstances you were trying to get away from? Sometimes teenagers (all of us, probably, at some point) don't realize that they can't run away from a problem. It's tempting to think that a boyfriend will rescue you from an intolerable situation at home, but without understanding why something went on, the teenager is often bound to replicate the situation in her new family. Pregnancy rarely gets you out of a mess. More often than not, it creates a whole new set of problems.

Some girls think that a baby will give them the love they never received. It doesn't work that way. The baby wants his own needs met; he has no concept of yours.

Some guys think a steady girl and a baby will bring a semblance of security and belonging. What they often find later is that they've forfeited their chances to build a career or go to college. The demands of providing an income for their family will drain them of the energy needed to pursue other interests.

Perhaps you genuinely believe your pregnancy was an accident. After all, you hadn't meant to go quite so far that night at the drive-in. Let me tell you, with that kind of thinking, it's only a matter of time before you get pregnant again. If you're old enough to be intimate with someone, you're certainly old enough to keep from having a baby out of the experience.

Don't even think it can't happen to you again. You didn't exactly plan that first one, did you?

CHAPTER 16

Questions to Ask

Yourself Before...*

A. Considering Marriage

1. Is the father of your unborn child someone you want to spend the next thirty years with?

2. How do you *both* feel about disciplining a child? Do you believe in spanking? in verbally threatening the child? Can you think of any circumstances in which you would strike your child?

3. What do you *both* think about earning, spending, and saving money?

4. Are you planning to stay at home with your child only temporarily? Do you *both* agree on when you should begin work? Will you need more education, and how will you get it?

---

*The questions are designed around the girl's experience, but they are equally pertinent for the guy simply by rephrasing them to fit his experience.

5. How many children do you *both* want?
6. What type of family life have you *both* been exposed to?
7. How much family support do you have now?
8. How are you going to spend family holidays?
9. How flexible is your spouse-to-be?
10. How does he relate to children? How do you?

B. Considering Abortion
1. Why do you feel unable to carry this child?
2. Have you talked this over with your boyfriend?
3. Do you know a reputable clinic or doctor to perform the abortion?
4. Do you have the money?
5. Do you have a support person to go through the experience with you?
6. Are you opting for abortion to please someone else or out of fear?
7. Is this a decision you can live with the rest of your life?
8. Do you know whom to turn to if you have regrets or guilt?

C. Considering Adoption
1. Have you looked into the various types of adoption agencies, and are you satisfied that what you're doing is best for you and the baby?
2. Can you live with the possibility of never seeing your child again?
3. Can you live with the reality that another woman will be "Mommy" to your child?
4. Are you willing to face the possibility that the child will look you up one day and not understand why you gave him or her away?
5. If you aren't ready for permanent adoption, have

you considered temporary foster care?

6. Do you care that your boyfriend or his family might choose to adopt the baby themselves?

D. Considering Single Parenthood

1. How much do you know about infants?
2. Do you have any real-life experience with them?
3. Do you have any adult to turn to if you become overwhelmed when things don't go as planned?
4. How do you plan to calm a cranky baby?
5. How will you maintain a social life?
6. Where will you live, and how will you support yourselves? For how long?
7. What hobbies or interests do you have? How will you maintain them?
8. How will you see to it that your baby gets adequate medical care?
9. What will you do if you're not a good mother?
10. Do you know CPR and the Heimlich maneuver? Can you handle a medical emergency?

E. Giving Up Your Education

1. If you're dropped out of school, how are you planning to support yourself the rest of your life?
2. If you're married, what will you do for money should your husband die or desert you?
3. If you think you might one day return to school, how will you manage it (child care, cost, time)?
4. What type of job or career would you like to hold if money weren't an obstacle?
5. What do you see yourself doing five years, ten years down the road?

F. Giving Up Your Friends

1. How important are your current friends?
2. What do you have in common with them?

3. Do you have any other friends in similar circumstances?
4. Whom do you have besides your immediate family for company?
5. Do your friends use drugs or alcohol?
6. Do you?
7. Can you stop?

G. Disclaiming Your Family
1. How much family support do you have?
2. Has your own childhood been chaotic (scary or confusing because of financial instability; sexual, physical, or sustance abuse?)
3. How do you plan to make a more peaceful life for yourself right now?
4. How have you dealt with your past?

H. Embarking on Pregnancy
1. Can you discuss all your fears with your doctor?
2. Do you know what to expect during labor and delivery?
3. Do you have someone trusted to go through childbirth with you?
4. Have you considered several options for medicinal relief if you're unwilling or unable to go through with an unmedicated birth? Do you even know what options are available?

I. Becoming a Mother or Father
1. Do you have a concerned adult you can turn to if you become overwhelmed with child-care responsibilities?
2. Will you have any opportunity to get out by yourself?
3. How will you afford all the things your baby needs?
4. What will you do if your baby won't stop crying? Is

choking? Isn't breathing?

5. Have you had any previous experience with infants? Have you taken any safety courses? Baby classes?
6. How do you plan to prevent future pregnancies?
7. How much do you know about STDs and AIDS? How do you intend not to contract them?

J. You Get Pregnant Again

1. What do you think are good reasons to have a baby?
2. What do you think are bad reasons?
3. How old do you think a person should be before becoming sexually active?
4. How old do you think a person should be before becoming a parent?
5. Is marriage important in raising a child?
6. How many children do you want to have?
7. How many can you afford?
8. Do you know why you chose to become pregnant in the first place?
9. Were there any family circumstances you were trying to escape?
10. Have those circumstances changed?

Bibliography

Bell, Ruth, et al. *Changing Bodies, Changing Lives*. New York: Vintage Books, 1988.

Bender, David, and Bruno Leone, eds. *Teenage Sexuality*. Minnesota: Greenhaven Press, 1988.

Benson, Michael. *Coping with Birth Control*. New York: The Rosen Publishing Group, 1988.

The Boston Women's Health Book Collective. *The New Our Bodies, Ourselves*. The Boston Women's Health Book Collective, 1984.

Goodman, Eric. "Men and Abortion" in *Glamour*, July 1989.

The Governor's Task Force. *Adolescent Pregnancy, A Framework for Prevention and Parenting*. Maine, 1986.

Hurley, Dan. "Why Are Our Babies Dying?" in *McCalls*, June 1989.

Johnson, Eric. *Love and Sex in Plain Language*. New York: Harper and Row, 1985.

Kurland, Adrienne. *Coping with Being Pregnant*. New York: The Rosen Publishing Group, 1988.

Pennetti, Michael. *Coping with School Age Fatherhood*. New York: The Rosen Publishing Group, 1988.

Bradley, Patricia, and Minor, Nancy. *Coping with School Age Motherhood*. New York: The Rosen Publishing Group, 1988.

Salholz, Eloise, et al. "The Future of Abortion" in *Newsweek*, July 17, 1989.

Index